WISDOM FOR FINANCIAL SUCCESS

From a Biblical Perspective

By
Francine E. Shaw

Published by

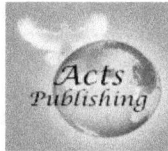

Acts
Publishing

Published by:
Act Publishing
P.O. Box 03600
Highland Park, MI 48203 USA

Bold comments within brackets noted in scripture are emphasis added by author. Take note that the name satan and associated names are not capitalized. We choose not to give him any preeminence, even to the point of violating grammatical rules.

Author: Francine E. Shaw
Cover Design: *Acts* Creative Team
Editor: *Acts* Editorial Team

First U.S. Edition Year 2011, 2nd Printing February 2013, 3rd Printing February 2017

Publisher's Cataloging-In-Publication Data

Shaw, Francine E.

Wisdom For Financial Success, From a Biblical Perspective
Financial principles and practices for victorious Christian Living

10 Digit ISBN 0-9861767-3-7 Perfect Bound Soft Cover
13 Digit ISBN 978-0-9861767-3-9 Perfect Bound Soft Cover

1. Christianity, Personal Finance

For current information about releases by Francine E. Shaw or other releases
Contact: *Acts Publishing,* P. O. Box 03600, Highland Park, MI 48203

Printed in the United States of America

v9 02 11 2017

Dedicated To

The Awesome Power of God

His Son, Jesus Christ and the Holy Spirit

Father, Mother, and Pop
Robert Perry (deceased), Ella L. Turner (deceased)
and Tenzly Turner Sr.

Husband
Ronald G. Shaw

My Three Daughters
Katrina K. Lyman-Pittman, Felicia A. Gayle,
Karimeh M. Lyman

Grandchildren
Anthony and Anna Pittman, Donovan Gayle and
Doshanay Lyman

Son-In-Laws
Anthony Pittman, and Donald Gayle

All of my Uncles and Aunts (living and deceased)

All my Sisters and Brothers
Especially Barbra Ann and Willie J. Lyman
(both deceased)

All of my Nieces and Nephews

Pastor Robert Bullard Jr. and the Bullard Family
Brother Harold Clayton

Pastor J. C. Powell (deceased) and Sister Geneva Powell
and the New World Community Church Family

Dedication cont.

Pastor Charles Kirby, Reverend Kenneth Phillips and
Pastor John Williams (deceased)

Deacon Harold Jerry and Sister Loretta Brown (deceased)

Bishop William Hamiliton France Sr. (deceased)
and Family
Mrs. Beulah Crockett (deceased)

Pastor Nathaniel Cotton Sr. and Sister Alice Cotton
and the Southern Christian Church Family

Reverend Sylvia Thames and
Pastor Clara Washington

Best Friend, Prayer Partner, Co-worker,
Etta Denise James (deceased)
Pastor Dwight L. Evans (deceased)

Deacon Carl Jones and Elizabeth Jones (deceased)

God Families
The Davis', The Nelson's, and The Neely's

Last but not least
Pastor Dewitt Matlock, Jr. of New Strength Ministries
Who spoke a word of prophecy concerning the writing
of this book, in December 2008.

Thank you all for shaping my life!
And to all who Trust in God's Wonderful Providence.

WISDOM FOR FINANCIAL SUCCESS

From a Biblical Perspective

By
Francine E. Shaw

Table of Contents

Preface.. XI
Introduction.. 1

Section I -
Get Wisdom; Get Understanding

Chapter 1 The Kingdom of God.............................. 16
Chapter 2 The Economy of God............................. 28
Chapter 3 Understanding the Tithe....................... 40

Section II -
Becoming Financially Successful

Chapter 4 Wisdom Defined..................................... 50
Chapter 5 Financial Success Defined.................... 62
Chapter 6 Becoming Financially Successful.......... 74

Section III -
Steps to Financial Freedom

Chapter 7 Step One - Trusting God........................ 90
Chapter 8 Step Two - Living Within One's Means..101
Chapter 9 Step Three - Giving...............................112

Section IV Epilogue

Bonus Prophetic Teaching From the Author
These Last Days...118

About the Author..129
.

-Preface-

I was shown a vision in 1986, and in the vision, I saw a multitude of people who were in their homes, crying out to God for deliverance. I was living in the city of Highland Park, Michigan at the time God spoke, and said that I had come from among them. Along with the vision was given mandate and a prophetic word. To prophesy is much more than predicting future events.

"A prophecy contains God's Word to the people, calling them to a covenant of faithfulness. The prophet's message is conditional and depends on the people's response. Thus, by their response to God's Word, the people greatly determine what their future holds. This book is written in response to the multitude that was shown to me in the vision in 1986. Its purpose is to teach us how to trust God in these last days." *(Adapted from: An Expository Dictionary of Biblical Words, Nashville: Thomas Nelson Publishers, 1894, pp 310-311).

I remember praying Psalm 51, and these words stayed in my heart:

Behold, thou desirest truth in the inward parts: and in the hidden part thou shalt make me to know wisdom. Purge me with hyssop, and I shall be clean: wash me, and I shall be whiter than snow. Make me to hear joy and gladness; that the bones which thou hast broken may rejoice. Hide thy face from my sins, and blot out all mine iniqui-ties. Create in me a clean heart, O God; and renew a right spirit within me. Cast me not away from thy presence; and take not thy holy spirit from me. Restore unto me the

joy of my salvation; and uphold me with thy
free spirit. Then will I teach transgressors
thy ways; and sinners shall be converted
unto thee (Psalm 51:6-13).

My first encounter with God was at the age of six years old. When I went to church with a woman by the name of Louise. She had given me a pouch with tie strings, and in it I believe were pennies for my offering to God. The message I heard not only prompted me to give God my offering, but I gave Him also my heart. From that day forward, I knew God was with me, and wherever we would move. I would always meet a friend whose family went to church, and I would always go with them. It was at the age of sixteen, that I met my oldest daughter's father, and conceived my first child. I had promised my Grandmother before she died, that I would finish high school. So, I was led by God to a school for ex pecting mothers, where I completed the eleventh grade, then returning to high school, I graduated in 1971. I celebrated my graduation in a nightclub, and carousing that night was a continuation of my backslidden condition.

Between the ages of seventeen and twenty-four sin had darkened my understanding so, that I was in bondage to alcohol. At this time, I had no knowledge of spiritual warfare. But, having knowledge of God's love, mercy and forgiveness (1 John 1:9). I began crying out to God for deliverance.

One evening in 1976, the Holy Spirit turned me into a tent revival, which was held at Brunette Baptist Church on the corner of 28th street, where I lived at that time. Before repenting at the age of twenty-four, I would wake up to a drink, and fall asleep with a drink. I began as a problem drinker. Whenever I had a problem I could not deal with or handle I would drink.

I had moved into my first apartment while on assistance at the age of twenty, and was not very responsible. So, life itself became a problem, and I began to wallow in self-pity.

-Preface-

At the time of the revival I had moved back home with my mother. I was on my way to the store for another drink, and as I walked pass the church, I found myself on my knees at the altar, repenting. I had been crying out to God in my drunken stupor the evening when this happened. At that time I did not trust anyone, let alone God, and from that day forward, God personally brought me through recovery, delivered me, and I began to grow spiritually, in spite of being confronted by the evil works of the devil.

The Prophetic Word I received for the people of God, is for us to not put our trust in this world's system, but for us to trust the Lord completely by surrendering our will to God: "That the demise of this nation will not come from a nuclear attack, or an invading army; nor a revolution, neither a terrorist attack. But, from an economic collapse, we have never seen before." God is calling the church to return to Him, so that we may prepare ourselves for the events which will lead up to the total collapse of this nation's economy.

The economy will look seemly well, and then suddenly the bottom will drop from under this nation. For those who can perceive, God has been showing us that man is not in control. But guess what? We are not under this economy. We are under the economy of God. It will not affect those who are trusting, and honoring the sovereign authority and power of God. God is calling us to live a life of total surrender. Yielding ourselves to the Holy Spirit, which is given to us for our sanctification. The Holy Spirit is the one who will separate us from the corruption that is in the world through lust. Therefore, we are called to walk after the Spirit, and not the flesh (Romans 8:114). This simply means that we are to follow the prompting of the Holy Spirit who will lead us into all truth (John 14:16-17). We are to follow Jesus, and not the course of this world, which is a course of destruction. Jesus prayed to the Father in John 17:13-19 saying:

*And now come I to thee; and these things I
speak in the world, that they might have my
joy fulfilled in themselves. I have given them
thy word; and the world hath hated them, because they are not of the world, even as I am
not of the world. I pray not that thou shouldest take them out of the world, but that thou
shouldest keep them from evil. They are not
of the world, even as I am not of the world.
Sanctify them through thy truth: thy word
is truth. As thou hast sent me into the world,
even so have I also sent them into the world.
And for their sakes I sanctify myself, that they
also might be sanctified through the truth.*

God's people lost sight of God during the time of their
prosperity, and slowly drifted back into the world and its
course only to find themselves in sinful lusts, and knee deep
in debt, which is bondage. The rug was pulled from under
many, now they must learn to live in total dependency on
God, not losing sight of what is going to happen amid this
climate of economic woes. In doing so, all who obey, God
will prosper them. Proverbs 29:2 tells us that:

*When the righteous are in authority, the
people rejoice: but when the wicked beareth
rule, the people mourn.*

During the Bush Administration, many people were
mourning. But now, is a time of preparation and rejoicing
for the people of God, for there have been a shift in the leadership of the nation, and the church (Daniel 2:19-23). Those
whom God have had hid on the backside of the mountain in
clefts, will slowly arrive on the scene preaching and teaching
the Gospel of the kingdom of God.

I recognize the gift of wisdom, and discernment in my life. The God given ability or power to live life skillfully, or to apply knowledge skillfully to life, and the ability or power to see, perceive, and or understand spiritual things, or the spiritual thing of God. God has allowed me to see, and understand the progression of my growth, in order for me to teach how we are to trust Him in these last days. I was shown a progression of growth. Progression means, a continuous connected series. The progression is Spiritual Awareness, Spiritual Warfare, and Spiritual Growth. Spiritual Awareness is becoming aware of the activities, or reality of the spiritual realm, or walking in the realm of the Spirit. Spiritual warfare is implementing the word of God, in defeat of the enemy, and Spiritual Growth is the process of sanctification; resulting in holiness.

A mandate is an authoritative order handed down from God. When heard we either heed it, or not. We will not be able to say to God that we were not warned. The mandate is for the people of God to return to the LORD. This mandate is not only for the people of God, but also for the world. God, before bringing judgment upon a people, nation, or individual, will always warn and give them space to repent (Jonah 1:1-2). The mandate is to bring God's tithe into the storehouse, the present day church, because the tithe honors the sovereign authority and power of God (Malachi 3:7-12). We give the tithe recognizing that our allegiance is to God, and that the earth, and all that is within the earth belongs to the LORD. We are not even our own. Psalm 24:1 says:

> *The earth is the LORD'S, and the fullness thereof; the world and they that dwell therein.*

The purpose of the tithe is for man to learn the fear of the LORD, and for the work of the ministry in the earth. It provides for God's place of worship, those working in the ministry, and the poor (Deuteronomy 14:22-29) God has not changed. He is the same yesterday, today, and forever (Hebrews 13:8). What has changed in the world today is the culture, time, and the terminology.

God's judgment will begin with the house of God first, and then the nations. 1 Peter 4:17-19 says:

> *For the time is come that judgment must begin at the house of God: and if it first begin at us, what shall the end be of them that obey not the gospel of God? And, **if the righteous scarcely be saved, where shall the ungodly and the sinner appear?** Wherefore let them that suffer according to the will of God commit the keeping of their souls to him in well doing, as unto a faithful Creator.*

We have forgotten the principles of God, which the founding father's established our nation upon. Psalm 9:17-18 says:

> *The wicked shall be turned into hell, and all the nations that forget God. For the needy shall not always be forgotten: the expectation **[or hope]** of the poor shall not perish for ever.*

Why? There is a shift, and God is calling the poor who are rich in faith, to seek His face. James the apostle says:

> *Listen my beloved brethren: Has God not chosen the poor of this world to be rich in*

*faith and heirs of the kingdom which He
promised to those who love Him (James 2:5
NKJV)?*

Love is the factor to obeying God, intentional obedience.
If we truly love God, we would no longer fulfill the lust of
the flesh. We would desire the things of God, and grow into
spiritual maturity. This will not happen if our total focus is
not on growing in the grace and knowledge of our Lord, Jesus Christ! The Apostle Peter says in 2 Peter 3:17-18,

> *Ye therefore, beloved, seeing ye know these
> things before, beware lest ye also, being led
> away with the error of the wicked, fall from
> your own steadfastness. But grow in grace,
> and in the knowledge of our Lord and Sav-
> ior Jesus Christ. To him be glory both now
> and for ever. Amen.*

Isaiah 55:6-9 goes on to warn us by saying:

> *Seek ye the LORD while he may be found,
> call ye upon him while he is near: Let the
> wicked forsake his way, and the unrigh-
> teous man his thoughts: and let him return
> unto the LORD, and he will have mercy
> upon him; and to our God, for he will abun-
> dantly pardon. For my thoughts are not
> your thoughts, neither are your ways my
> ways, saith the LORD. [Is] God does not
> contradict His word. God will never leave
> nor forsake us. But, we leave and forsake
> God. He says*

> *So shall my word be that goeth forth out of
> my mouth: it shall not return unto me void,
> but it shall accomplish that which I please,
> and it shall prosper in the thing whereto I*

sent it (Isaiah 55:11).

The divine favor of the LORD is given to all who love and honor Him. Those who seek Him for the wisdom, knowledge and understanding needed to become obedient to his will. Proverbs 8: 33-35 says:

> *Hear instruction, and be wise, and refuse it not. Blessed is the man that heareth me, watching daily at my gates, waiting at the posts of my doors. For whoso findeth me fin deth life, and shall obtain favor of the LORD* (Proverbs 8:17-21; Proverbs 10:22)

When we neglect to give our tithe to the church, which is the body of Christ, and the kingdom of God. We rob God, and are dishonoring Him. Malachi 3:8-10 asks us this question:

> *Will a man rob God? Yet ye have robbed me. But ye say, Wherein have we robbed thee? In tithes and offerings. Ye are cursed with a curse: for ye have robbed me, even this whole nation. Bring ye all the tithes into the storehouse, that there may be meat in mine house, and prove me now herewith, saith the LORD of hosts, if I will not open you the windows of heaven, and pour you out a blessing, that there shall not be room enough to receive it.*

God challenges us to prove or test Him, and while we are testing Him. He says, I will turn back the devourer from bringing you to financial ruins, and in your faithfulness. I will open the windows of heaven, and pour you out a blessing, that there shall not be room enough to receive it, God is speaking of a continual flow of His blessing upon us. We must understand that tithing from the net pay is not honoring God. Uncle Sam, takes his from the top. Otherwise, he too would not get what he feels belongs to him, taxes!

So the tithe belongs to the LORD, and is a spiritual mark of God. The visible sign that we trust Him. God gives marks for the purpose of identifying something or someone (Genesis 4:15; Ezekiel 9:4-7; Romans 16:17-20).

The offering, on the other hand, is what gives us the increase. The Apostle Paul in 2 Corinthians 9:6-8 says:

> *But this I say, He which soweth sparingly shall reap also sparingly; and he which soweth bountifully shall reap also bountifully. Every man according as he purposeth in his heart, so let him give; not grudgingly, or of necessity: for God loveth a cheerful giver. And God is able to make all grace abound toward you; that ye, always having all sufficiency in all things, may abound to every good work: (As it is written, **he hath dispersed abroad; he hath given to the poor: his righteousness remaineth for ever)***

Paul continues to explain that giving is an administration of service to the poor, and that God not only supplies seed to the sower, but He supplies our food from the seed sown, and that He also increases the fruits of our righteousness (2 Corinthians 9:10-15).

This mandate originated in Malachi 3:6-10, and is in effect to this day. In Romans chapter eleven, the Apostle Paul speaks about the restoration of Israel and that the blindness of Israel happened in part until the fullness of the Gentiles would come. The mystery that Paul is speaking about is this,

> *And so all Israel shall be saved: as it is writ-*
> *ten,* **there shall come out of Zion the**
> **deliverer, and shall turn away un-**
> **godliness from Jacob: for this is my**
> **covenant unto them, when I shall take**
> **away their sins** (Romans 11:26)

The Apostle Paul is speaking of Jesus Christ, the deliverer. Malachi 3:7-8 goes on say:

> *For I am the LORD, I change not; therefore*
> *ye sons of Jacob are not consumed. Even*
> *from the days of your fathers ye are gone*
> *away from my ordinances, and have not*
> *kept them. Return unto me, and I will re-*
> *turn unto you, saith the LORD of hosts. But*
> *ye said, Wherein shall we return? Will a*
> *man rob God?*

Yes, God's people, who are Abraham's seed, are yet robbing God, those of us who are not honoring Him with the tithe. The Apostle Paul explains the mystery further by saying:

> *As concerning the gospel, they are enemies*
> *for your sakes;* (Romans 11:28a).

The sons of Jacob are enemies of God for our sake. But, as touching the election which we are, they are beloved of God for the father's sake, for the gifts and calling of God are without repentance, which means that the gifts are irrevocable. Our gifts and calling through faith operates, even in our disobedience concerning the giving of our tithe and offering (Romans 11:29). Paul now begins to speak about the new covenant when he says:

-Preface-

For as ye in times past have not believed
God, yet have now obtained mercy through
their unbelief (sons of Jacob): Even so have
these also now not believed (sons of Jacob),
that through your mercy they also my obtain
*mercy. **For God hath concluded them all***
in unbelief, that he might have mercy
***upon all.** O the depth of the riches both of*
the wisdom and knowledge of God! How un-
searchable are his judgments, and his ways
past finding out (Romans 11:30-33)!

We have not been consumed because of the mercy of
God, upon us the sons of Jacob, and we are to no longer walk
according to the course of this world, because Jesus Christ
has saved us (Romans 11:26) We are the seed of Abraham,
and God is calling us to return unto Him. When God spoke
of the father's sakes, He is speaking of Abraham, Isaac, and
Jacob. The promise of the new covenant that was made to
Israel. We have been engrafted into the vine, and were born
of God through the Spirit of adoption (John 15:5; Galatians
34:3-7). We are the other sheepfold Jesus is speaking of in
John 10:16 which says:

And other sheep I have, which are not of this
fold: them also I must bring, and they shall
hear my voice; and there shall be one fold,
and one shepherd.

Also, scripture says there is a book of remembrance
which is written and is before the Lord of them that feared
the Lord, and meditate on his name. Malachi 3:6-18 tells us
that we will be able to discern the righteous and the wicked,
between him that serve God and him that serve Him not
(Romans 8:15; 11:25-12:2).

Some churches have replaced the teaching of the tithe, with the new testament giving, using the scripture which says:

> *Now concerning the collection for the saints, as I have given order to the churches of Galatia, even so do ye. Upon the first day of the week let every one of you lay by him in store, as God hath prospered him, that there be no gatherings when I come. And when I come, whomsoever ye shall approve by your letters, them will I send to bring your liberality unto Jerusalem* (1 Corinthians 16:1-3).

But, the scripture in 2 Corinthians 9:1 that says:

> *For as touching the ministering to the saints, it is superfluous for me to write to you.*

Refutes this teaching as it explains that Paul had given orders to the churches at Galatians, and Macedonia asking for contributions for the poor saints at Jerusalem, which the Corinth church had pledged first, provoking the other churches to give. So Paul writes to them of his boasting of their liberality encouraging them to have their collection ready when he comes. His encouragement to them was the attitude in which they were to give, and that if they would give generously, they would reap bountifully. These scriptures clearly show that these collections were purposed for the necessities of the poor saints at Jerusalem, who had forsaken all to follow Christ. Therefore, have nothing to do with replacing the tithe, which is to be given to the church. God has already given us the command in the amount we are to give toward the work of the Kingdom of God!

We all can afford to give God our tithes. It's a matter of us prioritizing our expenditures, and spending our income wisely. Our income is progressive, as with our growth. Our growth depends on our willingness to obey God's Word. Likewise, God will take what we have, and increase our portion as we obey Him. God prospers us according to our faith, obedience, trust, and our living wise, all is what enables us to give God the tithe.

As a result of our selfishness, we are bringing shame to the church when we have clothing hung out front and alongside of some churches. We are bringing shame to the church when we have barbecue and fish fry signs posted outside of some churches. We are sending the wrong message to the world. God has already provided for the work of the ministry. Scripture says:

> *There is a way which seemeth right unto a man, but the end thereof are the ways of death* (Proverbs 14:12).

God says:

> *Ye are cursed with a curse; for ye have robbed me, even this whole nation* (Malachi 3:9).

God is calling us to return to Him, by bringing the tithe into the storehouse. I truly believe in my heart, as we individually return unto the Lord, the wealth of the wicked will be released upon the body of Christ, the Church. Proverbs 13:22 says:

> *A good man leaveth an inheritance to his children's children: and the wealth of the sinner is laid up for the just.*

Our inheritance is in God, and He is good.

As we look at the pledge of allegiance, to the flag of the United States of America it says, "to the republic for which it stands, one nation, under God, indivisible, with liberty and justice for all. Then, on our currency we have "In God we trust." Yet, are we really trusting God? Many trust in the paper that these very words are written on, and those of us who are not tithing are robbing God, and that makes us thieves. When Jesus cleanse the temple in Mark 11:15-19, verse seventeen says: *"And he taught saying unto them, is it not written, My house shall be called of all nations the house of prayer? But ye have made it a den of thieves."*

Notice that Malachi 3:1-5 speaks about the approach of the Day of Judgment. Malachi 3:6-18 speaks about the payments of tithes. Malachi 4:1-6 speaks about the coming day of the Lord. When John the Baptist came on the scene, there had been 400 years of silence. He came preaching repentance. I challenge you to read these scriptures, and pray for God to give you the spirit of wisdom and revelation in the knowledge of Jesus Christ, that the eyes of your understanding be enlightened so that you may know what is the hope of His calling, and what the riches of the glory of his inheritance in the saints (Ephesians 1:17-18) Repent, for the Kingdom of God is at hand (Ephesians 1:15-19; Luke 3:4-9)!

✝

—Introduction—

Wisdom for Financial Success from a Biblical Perspective is a book that will give you the insight and the understanding of the kingdom of God, the economy of God, along with the law of the tithe, and how trusting God, living within one's means, and giving to others will bring true contentment. The intent of this book is to help you to expand your perception, so that you can see from a biblical perspective. Why? And what causes so many of the people of God, to seek after the seen, and temporal, rather than the unseen, and eternal?

Proverbs 3:5-6 says:

> *Trust in the LORD with all thine heart; and*
> *lean not unto thine own understanding. In*
> *all thy ways acknowledge him, and he shall*
> *direct thy paths.*

When we truly trust the Lord with our whole heart, and lean or depend not on your own understanding, but allow the Holy Spirit to give us wisdom, knowledge and under-standing. Scripture says that the Lord will lead and direct our path as we acknowledge the sovereign authority and power of God in our lives.

The psalmist then tells us that our path will be lead and directed by the Lord, who is able to show us what, when and how to do God's will. We have the Holy Spirit residing in us, to help us live holy and righteous lives. Otherwise, we would not be able to live the life God is calling us to live. Many would be surprised at my past, because it took trust-ing God to bring me through the things I have experienced. God has changed my life entirely, these last five years of my seeking Him, and I have surrender completely to God. Sa-tan literally has tried to destroy me, and would have, had I not been on the Lord side. He will try to discredit our lives by digging up our past (mark my words), because he does not want us to know the truth.

Its okay, because we should not be ashamed of the Gospel of Jesus Christ, for it is the power of God unto salvation. From the time I repented, to the surrender of my will, God has help me. God has helped me to overcome self, the practice of sin and the wiles of the devil through prayer, the power of the Holy Spirit, and the obedient act of my will. I am now aware, that the times I stumbled and fell, were the times I allowed anger to come into my heart. We are to:

> *Put on the whole armor of God, that ye may be able to stand against the wiles of the devil. For we wrestle not against flesh and blood, but against principalities, against powers, against the rulers of the darkness of this world, against spiritual wickedness in high places* (Ephesians 6:11-12).

The wiles of the devil are attacks against the mind, which is the battlefield where spiritual warfare is waged. Wiles are cunning strategies. The devil's purpose and plans are to take our focus from God, and to put it on other things. Wiles defined is, "to trick or entice somebody into doing or not doing something." Anger is the most destructive wile of the devil. We are not to allow anger to come into our hearts. Proverbs 4:23 says, *"Keep thy heart with all diligence; for out of it are the issues of life."*

Issues are subjects of concern, a source of conflict, mis giving, or emotional distress. Issues that are not dealt with, or are unresolved will lay dominant in our hearts, and when (tricked) or triggered, will surface. Its called displaced emotion or aggression, and over a period of time, if accumulated, will cause us to say or do something we otherwise would not have done. Aggression is the destruction that we see in the world today. I believe envy is the second wile of the devil (Proverbs 14:30). Satan's evil forces will take hold of anger, and ruin the very life of those who open that door to sin. Ephesians 4:26 says:

> *Be ye angry, and sin not: let not the sun*
> *go down upon your wrath: Neither give*
> *place to the devil.*

We are told this for a specific reason. Anger in the heart gives place to the devil, and will cause, as with any other negative emotions that are not dealt with, that lay dominant in our hearts, and when triggered to surface. God has taught me how not to internalize my negative feelings and how to guard my heart and mind by making me aware of the spiritual attacks of the enemy on my life through discernment. The Apostle Paul even tells us that God will keep (guard) our hearts and minds, through Christ Jesus as we give ourselves to prayer, and supplication, giving thanks unto the Father (Philippians 4:6-7).   Becoming aware of spiritual warfare is what will help us overcome and resolve the problems and circumstances so many of us are faced with today. This is why it is so important for us to not only be a hearer of the word, but we must also be a doer of the word because faith without works is dead (Ephesians 6:11-18; James 2:26) and walking in the truth of God's word is what defeats the devil, intentional obedience.

The true believer who is born of God's Spirit, is a citizen of the kingdom of God, and I will be sharing the basic truths contributing to becoming financially successful, from a Bib lical perspective. So many of God's people are seeking those things that are seen, and temporal, rather then the things that are unseen, and eternal (Colossians 3:1-4:6).

What is true discipleship? Scripture gives us a true defi nition of discipleship. John 8:31-32 says:

> *Then said Jesus to those Jews which believed on him, If ye continue in my word, then are ye my disciples indeed; and ye shall know the truth, and the truth shall make you free.*

First of all, the truth will make us free from the power of sin in our lives, which power we receive through salvation. Secondly, the truth will make us free from the bondage of fear, worry, anxiety, and the cares of this world, as we come to know and trust God. Third, the truth of God's word will give us the freedom we need to fellowship with our Lord, Jesus Christ, and to worship God, the Father our Creator.

The word disciple means someone who believes, and helps spread the doctrine or teachings of another. John the Baptist was the forerunner of Jesus Christ, and he came preaching the baptism of repentance for the remission of sins (Mark 1:4). The doctrine of the Kingdom of God, or the Kingdom of Heaven, which is interchangeable, is what Jesus preached. Mark 1:14-15 says:

> *Now after that John was put in prison, Jesus came into Galilee, preaching the gospel of the kingdom of God. And saying, The time is fulfilled, and the kingdom of God is at hand: repent ye, and believe the gospel.*

He then called to Himself his disciples, and taught them kingdom living. You will also find in Luke 4:43 Jesus saying, after healing many in Capernaum,

> *I must preach the kingdom of God to other cities also: for therefore am I sent.*

-Introduction-

The principles of kingdom living, taught by Jesus to His disciples and the multitudes are found throughout the book of Matthew, and the other gospels. The Sermon on the Mount is where Jesus made known the blessing bestowed upon all who would enter into God's kingdom. He spoke of God's people as the light of the world, and that obedience is necessary for kingdom living (1 Peter 2:9-10). Jesus spoke these words in Matthew 7:21-23 saying:

> *Not every one that saith unto me, Lord, Lord, shall enter into the kingdom of heaven; but he that doeth the will of my Father which is in heaven. Many will say to me in that day, Lord, Lord, have we not prophesied in thy name? And in thy name have cast out devils? And in thy name done many wonderful works? And then will I profess unto them, I never knew you: depart from me, ye that work iniquity.*

Workers of iniquity are those who have not done work according to God's will, but according to their own will. Who fail to know, hear, or wait on the voice of the Lord before doing his supposedly work in the earth. Jesus gave us authority to use His name.

> *... In my name shall they cast out devils; they shall speak with new tongues; They shall take up serpents; and if they drink any deadly thing, it shall not hurt them; they shall lay hands on the sick, and they shall recover* (Mark 16:17-18).

He said these signs shall follow them that believe. James 2:19 says:

> *Thou believest that there is one God; thou doest well: the devils also believe, and tremble.*

We possess saving faith to enact upon the truth of God's word. The apostle James is saying to us that the devils have enough sense even though they do not posses saving faith, to tremble at the truth of God's word. And, in the wrong hands, Jesus' name is being use for the wrong motives.

False prophets and teachers are preaching and teaching another gospel causing many to believe supposedly that godliness is gain, that it is the means to become wealthy. But the apostle Paul tells Timothy, that godliness with contentment is great gain (1 Timothy 6:5-6). There are also some who are promoting godliness as a means of profit, causing people to become covetous, rather then them pursuing God. The result for many is that they are poor toward God in spiritual things, and lack the true wisdom, knowledge, and understanding needed to grow spiritually mature. Many Christians are accumulating material possessions, only to remain in darkness, and are not shining as lights in the world.

I knew what living a saved life was at a young age. I knew how it felt to not blend in with my peers, because of my godly morals, and values. I knew what it felt like to once have joy, and then sorrow dominating my life. I knew the condemnation of walking in darkness. Whenever I would sin while I was still in captivity of the devil. The Holy Spirit would convict me, and knowing that I served a forgiving God I would only confess my sins. To repent is to turn from sin, toward God. It is not enough to confess sin. We must turn away from sin, and be converted. Conversion is a change of mind, that results in a change of conduct.

-Introduction-

Our sinful conduct must change, and if we have not any desire at all, to live godly lives. We should question whether we are saved, because the convicting power of the Holy Spirit, will not allow us to remain in sin. God chastens those whom He loves, and will cause us to turn back to Him (Hebrews 12:6-11). Our problem comes when we hear, and do not obey. When we are rebelling against God, and do not obey Him. He then will allow adverse situations and circumstances to come into our lives to discipline us, and as the results of his chastening. We will then turn and repent.

> *Though He were a Son, yet learned he obedience by the things which he suffered; And being made perfect, he became the author of eternal salvation unto all them that obey him; call of God a high priest after the order of Melchizedek (Hebrews 5:8-10).*

The apostle Peter confirms, that when we have suffered enough, as the result of our disobedience we then will turn from our sins. He says:

> **Forsasmuch** *then as Christ hath suffered for us in the flesh, arm yourselves likewise with the same mind: for he that hath suffered in the flesh hath ceased from sin; That he no longer should live the rest of his time in the flesh to the lusts of men, but to the will of God [is] (1 Peter 4:1-2).*

When I turned from sin, I had suffered enough. John also tells us in 1 John 2:15 :

> *Love not the world, neither the things that are in the world. If any man love the world,*

*the love of the Father is not in him. For all
that is in the world, the lust of the flesh, and
the lust of the eyes, and the pride of life, is
not of the Father, but is of the world. And
the world passeth away, and the lust thereof: but he that doeth the will of God abideth
for ever.*

Romans 12:1, 2 talks about the will of God and says:

*I BESEECH you therefore, brethren, by the
mercies of God, that ye present your bodies
a living sacrifice, holy, acceptable unto God,
which is your reasonable service. And be not
conformed to this world: but be ye transformed by the renewing of your mind, that
ye may prove what is that good, and acceptable, and perfect, will of God.*

We must be born of the Spirit in order to enter the kingdom of God, and to abide; the word of God must abide in
us. If we are entangled in the world, confessing Christ, but
not abiding in his word, we need to be transformed by the
renewing of our mind (Romans 12:1-2). Why? Satan has deceived so many in believing they can live sinful lives, and
still enter into God's kingdom.

We must repent, and be born of the Spirit. Jesus told
Nicodemus,

*Verily, verily, I say unto thee, Except a man
be born again, he cannot enter the kingdom
of God* (John 3:3-8).

The definition of the word "enter" means, "to become a
participant; to be involved in; to enter an agreement." Jesus

is saying that the true believer or born-again Christian, being of the new birth, is now able to discern spiritual things or the spiritual things of God and now, have been made alive in Christ. We are now able to desire the growth we need to become mature. The Apostle Peter explains it like this in 1 Peter 2:2-3:

> As newborn babes, desire the sincere milk of the word, that ye may grow thereby: If so be ye have tasted that the Lord is gracious.

We must keep in mind that lust hinders spiritual growth, and desire initiates it. Jesus Christ did not die for us to continue in our sins.

> What shall we say then? Shall we continue in sin, that grace may abound? God forbid. How shall we, that are dead to sin, live any longer therein? (Romans 6:1-2)

John, the of son of Zebedee also says:

> Little children, let no man deceive you: he that do righteousness is righteous, even as he is righteous. He that committeth sin is (controlled) of the devil; for the devil sinneth from the beginning. For this purpose the Son of God was manifested, that he might destroy the works of the devil. Whosoever is born of God doth not commit sin; for his seed (word) remaineth in him: and he cannot sin, because he is born of God. In this the children of God are manifest, and the children of the devil: whosoever doeth not righteousness is not of God, neither he that loveth not his brother (1 John 3:7-10).

9

The reason so many professing to be born of God, are remaining in sin, is because they do not have the righteousness of God, which is from faith to faith, are not abiding in the truth, and the truth is not abiding in them, let along the scriptures, for in the scriptures are eternal life: as it is written, "the just shall live by faith." For the wrath of God is revealed from heaven against all ungodliness and unrighteousness of men; who hold the truth in unrighteousness. Which means that they know the truth, but are not abiding in the truth (Romans 1:17, 18). The true born-again believers, are those who have purified their soul in obeying the truth through the Spirit, and who love the brethren with a pure heart. Born again not of corruptible seed, but of incorruptible by the word of God, which live and abide forever (1 Peter 1:18-23).

God is calling us to live holy lives, and we are not hearing Him, because we refuse to mortify the flesh, and put its deeds to death. We love the pleasures of sin, and are not delighting ourselves in the LORD. We are told to delight ourselves in the LORD, and He will give us the desires of our hearts, to commit our way to Him, and trust, and He will bring it to pass (Psalm 37:4-7). Psalm 37:8 also tells us to cease from anger, and to forsake wrath. Why? Again, because we give place to the devil when we allow anger to enter or remain in our hearts. We are the people of God, and are commanded to walk in love.

There is more to salvation, then just professing the name of Jesus. We must repent, and turn from our sin. The apostle Peter, preaching on the day of Pentecost, uttered these words:

> *Repent, and be baptized every one of you in the name of Jesus Christ for the remission of sins, and ye shall receive the gift of the Holy*

Ghost. For the promise is unto you, and to your children, and to all that are afar off, even as many as the Lord our God shall call. Then they that gladly received his word were baptized: and the same day there were added unto them about three thousand souls. And they continued steadfastly in the apostles' (teachings) doctrine and fellowship, and in breaking of bread, and in prayers (Acts 2:38-39; 41-42).

Again Paul said,

What shall we say then? Shall we continue in sin, that grace may abound? God forbid. How shall we that are dead to sin, live any longer therein? Know ye not, that so many of us as were baptized into Jesus Christ were baptized into his death? Therefore are buried with him by baptism into death: that like as Christ was raised up from the dead by the glory of the Father, even so we also should walk in newness of life. For if we have been planted together in the likeness of his death, we shall be also in the likeness of his resurrection: Knowing this, that our old man (old nature) is crucified with him, that the body of sin might be destroyed, that henceforth we should not serve sin. For he that is dead is freed from sin. Now if we be dead with Christ, we believe that we shall also live with him: Knowing that Christ being raised from the dead dieth no more; death hath no more dominion over him. For in that he died, he died unto sin once: but in

11

that he liveth, he liveth unto God. Likewise reckon ye also yourselves to be dead indeed unto sin, but alive unto God through Jesus Christ our Lord. Let not sin therefore reign in your mortal body, that ye should obey it in the lusts thereof. Neither yield ye your members as instruments of unrighteousness unto sin: but yield yourselves unto God, as those that are alive from the dead, and your members as instruments of righteousness unto God (Romans 6:1-13).

Paul tells us that the old nature was put to death with Christ. But that sin yet reigns in our mortal body or flesh. We are now told to put to death our bodies, by yielding our bodies to God. We do this by resisting the lusts of our flesh, and yielding ourselves to God. Another scripture says:

Submit yourselves therefore to God. Resist the devil, **[temptation to fulfill our lusts]**, *and he will flee from you. Draw nigh to God, and he will draw nigh to you* (James 4:7-8a).

Jesus came to destroy the works of the devil, and to save us from the power of sin in our lives. Paul's warning in Hebrews 10:26-31, says:

For if we [is] **[Paul is speaking about the people of God]** *sin willfully after that we have received the knowledge of the truth, there remaineth no more sacrifice for sins, But a certain fearful looking for of judgment and fiery indignation, which shall devour the adversaries* **[our enemies].** *He that despised Moses' law died without mercy under two or three witnesses: Of how much sorer* *punishment, suppose ye, shall he be thought worthy, who hath trodden under foot the Son of God, and hath counted the blood of the covenant, wherewith he was sanctified, an unholy thing, and hath done despite unto the Spirit of grace? For we know him that hath said,* **vengeance belongeth unto me, I will recompense, saith the Lord. And again, the Lord shall judge his people.** *It is a fearful thing to fall into the hands of the living God.*

Therefore, we are told that we cannot serve two masters. Jesus uses the personification of wealth, as the other master, out of all the other things we put before God. Why? Wealth is God's chief competitor. The devil told Jesus in the wilderness when He was being tempted, that if He would fall down, and worship him he would give Him all the kingdoms of the world and their glory. Matthew 4:10 says:

Then saith Jesus unto him, Get thee hence, Satan: for it is written, ***thou shalt worship the Lord thy God, and him only shalt thou serve.***

The devil has rule over all who are walking in darkness, or sin. They are being deceived, because they do not believe the word of God. Paul says:

But if our gospel be hid, it is hid to them that are lost: In whom the god of this world hath blinded the minds of them which believe not, lest (unless) the light of the glorious gospel of Christ, who is the image of God, should shine unto them (2 Corinthians 4:3-4).

Satan who also is the god of this world, and is blinding the minds of all who do not believe, are lost, and are walking in darkness. Scripture says unless the light of the glorious gospel of Jesus Christ should shine unto them, they will remain in sin. So if you are confessing Jesus Christ as your savior, and are walking in disobedience, you are rebelling against God and need to repent, and be converted! And, if you are professing Jesus Christ, and are not saved, you need to ask God to forgive you, repent and be converted, because you are of the children of disobedience and the wrath of God is upon you (1 John 3:4-12).

Jesus in the Sermon on the Mount teaches us what our attitudes and dispositions should be concerning various issues of life, along with giving us tools to discipline ourselves (Matthew 6:1-18). These spiritual tools, or exercises, are giving, prayer, and fasting, which help develop in us trust, communion, and fellowship with God. Kingdom living is denying self, taking up our cross, and following Jesus. The key to understanding kingdom living is found in Colossians 1:9-14, in which the apostle Paul says:

> *For this cause we also, since the day we heard it, do not cease to pray for you, and to desire that ye might be filled with the knowledge of his will in* **all wisdom and spiritual understanding;** *That ye might walk worthy of the Lord, unto all pleasing, being fruitful in every good work, and increasing in the knowledge of God; Strengthened with all might, according to his glorious power, unto all patience and longsuffering with joyfulness; Giving thanks unto the Father, which hath made us meet to be partakers of the inheritance of the saints in light:* **Who hath delivered us from the power of darkness, and hath translated us into the kingdom of his dear Son: In whom we have redemption through his blood,**

even the forgiveness of sins.

Truly understanding our salvation is what brings us into the knowledge of God, to walk in obedience to his will. Therefore, we have not been saved to continue to walk in darkness, or disobedience. But we have been saved to walk and live worthy of our calling. What then qualifies us to be saints? Our faith in the Lord Jesus Christ, to which we are saved, and true knowledge of God, along with the acceptance of His Son, is what qualifies us to be saints, because Jesus teaches us how to trust Him (Proverbs 3:5-6). So, Jesus explains to us in Matthew, the sixth chapter, not to seek after wealth, but God. We are to pursue God, rather than pursue after the things we feel will make us happy. True happiness comes from God (Matthew 5:1-11). We are to seek to understand God's righteousness, seek to understand what the Kingdom of God is, and seek to understand God's providence. And the purpose of this book is to teach us how to trust God in these last days, and to help us grow in the grace and knowledge of our Lord, and Savior, Jesus Christ, that we may prosper in our finances.

✝

Section I

Get Wisdom; Get Understanding

—**1**—
The Kingdom of God

For the kingdom of God is not meat and drink;
But righteousness, and peace, and joy
In the Holy Ghost (Romans 14:17).

The kingdom of God defined, is the sovereign rule of God manifested in Christ to defeat his enemies, creating a people over whom He reigns, and ushering in a realm in which the power of his reign is experienced. It is the eternal sovereignty or kingly rule of God, manifested in its acceptance by men on earth, and the hope of the future. In simple terms, it is the rule and reign of God in the heart of the believer. Therefore, when Jesus says in Matthew 4:17b,

> *Repent: for the kingdom of heaven is at hand.*

He is not calling on his listeners to prepare for the coming of the kingdom. But, He was announcing that the kingdom is here. Understand that the kingdom blessings promised in Isaiah 35:110 are to be fulfilled in the future kingdom.

This announcement I am referring to in Matthew 4:17 was that of the spiritual coming of the kingdom. Jesus confirms this by saying in Matthew 12:28, to the Pharisees ac cusing Him of casting out devils by Beelzebub,

> *But if I cast out devils by the Spirit of God,*
> *then the kingdom of God is come unto you.*

So, when Jesus was demanded of the Pharisees when the kingdom of God should come, He told them:

> *...The kingdom of God cometh not with ob-*
> *servation: Neither shall they say, Lo here!*
> *or, lo there! For, behold, the kingdom of God*
> *is within you* (Luke 17:20b-21).

The kingdom of God is within you. It is not a physical kingdom. The words within you translates to mean: in the midst of you. Therefore, Jesus was telling the Pharisees that the kingdom of God has already come, and it did not come with observation. You cannot see the Kingdom of God, because it is not yet a physical kingdom, where Jesus is ruling and reigning on earth; this will happen after his second coming. At Jesus' first coming, He came as the Messiah, to save his people the Jews from their sins, but many rejected Him. They were looking for the promised King, Christ Himself, who would rule in righteousness. Someone who would overthrow the Roman government, and establish his physical kingdom on earth. Well, at his second coming, He will overthrow the governments of this world, and establish his physical kingdom. But right now, the kingdom of God is a spiritual kingdom, the present day church (Romans 14:17).

The kingdom of God is a nation, as was the nation of Israel in Biblical times. Even though they were under the rule of the Roman government, they had their own government. This was plainly seen when they came to Pointus Pilate seeking the death penalty for Jesus. John 18:31-36 says:

> *Then said Pilate unto them, Take ye him,*
> *and judge him according to your law. The*
> *Jews therefore said unto him, It is not law-*
> *ful for us to put any man to death: That the*
> *saying of Jesus might be fulfilled, which he*
> *spake, signifying what death he should die.*
> *Then Pilate entered into the judgment hall*
> *again, and called Jesus, and said unto him,*
> *Art thou the King of the Jews? Jesus answer*

> *him, Sayest thou this thing of thyself, or did*
> *others tell it thee of me? As sometimes He*
> *does, Jesus answers with a question, and*
> *[is] Pilate answered, Am I a Jew?* **Thine**
> **own nation** *and the chief priests have de-*
> *livered thee unto me: what hast thou done?*
> *Jesus answered, My kingdom is not of this*
> *world: if my kingdom were of this world,*
> *then would my servants fight, that I should*
> *not be delivered to the Jews: but now is my*
> *kingdom not from hence.*

Likewise, we are citizens of God's kingdom, who are under the leadership of other nations to which we have been saved out from among, and God is reigning in our hearts. God's kingdom has no boundaries; it exceeds race, creed, color, and nationality. So what exactly is the spiritual nature of God's kingdom, now present in the earth? To understand the kingdom of God, we must first understand the context of our salvation. Jesus not only died for our sins, but He came to deliver us from the power of sin and in the future, the very presence of sin. We have been deceived into believing that we do not have power over sin in our lives. But, we are told by the apostle Paul to thank God for what He has done through Jesus Christ, his Son. He says:

> *Giving thanks unto the Father, which hath*
> *made us meet to be partakers of the in-*
> *heritance of the saints in light:* **Who hath**
> **delivered us from the power of dark-**
> **ness, and hath translated us into the**
> **kingdom of his dear Son:** *In whom we*
> *have redemption through his blood, even*
> *the forgiveness of sins: Who is the image*
> *of the invisible God, the firstborn of every*
> *creature: For by him were all things cre-*

*ated, that are in heaven, and that are in
earth, visible and invisible, whether they be
thrones, or dominions, or principalities, or
powers: all things were created by him, and
for him: And he is before all things, and by
him all things consist. And he is the head
of the body, the church: who is the beginning, the firstborn from the dead; that in
all things he might have the preeminence.
For it pleased the Father that in him should
all fullness dwell; And, having made peace
through the blood of his cross, by him to rec-
oncile all things unto himself; by him, I say,
whether they be things in earth, or things in
heaven. And you, that were sometime alien-
ated and enemies in your mind by wicked
works, yet now hath he reconciled In the
body of his flesh through death, to present
you holy and unblamable and unreprovable
in his sight* (Colossians 1:12-22).

We have been made the righteousness of God, through
Jesus Christ, and are called to walk in our deliverance, and
to live holy lives.

The beatitude is a sermon on true Christian living, or the
lifestyle of the kingdom. It is a sermon on how we should
conduct ourselves, or on our conduct. The lifestyle of God's
kingdom is obedience, and doing the will of God. True spiritual living is an attitude of the heart. When we are walking
in obedience to the word of God we no longer allow anger, or
lust to control us. There is true commitment, forgiveness,
and love for God, one another, and our enemies. Jesus' time
spent on the earth doing the will of the Father included the
training, or disciplining, of his disciples. The word discipline means: training which corrects, molds, or perfects the
mental faculties or moral character; to correct poor behav-

ior; to train or develop by teaching and by control; to bring order; behavior which results from such training; obedience to authority or rules.

Paul says:

> *Let no man deceive you with vain* **[empty]** *words: for because of these things cometh the wrath of God upon the children of disobedience. Be not ye therefore partakers with them. For ye were sometimes darkness, but now are ye light in the Lord: walk as children of light: (For the fruit of the Spirit is in all goodness and righteousness and truth;) Proving what is acceptable unto the Lord. And have no fellowship with the unfruitful works of darkness, but rather reprove* **[expose]** *them. For it is a shame even to speak of those things* **[fornication, adultery, covetousness, homosexual acts, child molestation, rapes, beastality etc.]** *Which are done of them in secret. But all things that are reproved* **[expose]** *are made manifest by the light: for whatsoever doth make manifest is light. Wherefore he saith, Awake thou that sleepest, and arise from the dead, and Christ shall give thee light* (Ephesians 5:6-14).

When we sincerely accept Jesus Christ in our heart, by faith, we are saved, sealed, and translated into the kingdom of God. The word translated means: to remove from one place to another. We were removed from the world, and translated into the kingdom of God. The believer is now a citizen of God's Kingdom. This is what scripture means when it says, *"we are in the world, but not of the world."* 1 John 4:5-6 says:

*They are of the world: therefore speak they
of the world, and the world heareth them.
We are of God: he that knoweth God heareth
us; he that is not of God heareth not us.
Hereby know we the spirit of truth, and the
spirit of error.*

So then, the kingdom of God is the rule and reign of God
in the heart of the believer. God governs our hearts by His
righteousness, His peace, and His joy. Jesus, at this present time, is sitting on the right hand of God's throne. He is
interceding for us, and He is our advocate (Hebrews 12:2;
Mark 16:19; Hebrews 7:22-25; Hebrews 8:1).

We must understand that we still have our free will, so
our translation into the kingdom of God does not automati-
cally cause us to submit to God's rule. We must completely
surrender our will to God. Therefore, many of us are living
in rebellion. 1 John 5:17-21 says:

*All unrighteousness is sin: and there is a
sin not unto death* **[not accepting Jesus
Christ, and blaspheming the Holy Spirit is the sin unto death, all other sins we
can repent of and be reconciled].** *We
know that whosoever is born of God sinneth
not* **[habitual, deliberate and persis-
tent rebellion against God]***; but he that
is begotten of God keepeth himself, and that
wicked one toucheth him not. And we know
that we are of God, and the whole world lieth in wickedness. And we know that the
Son of God is come, and hath given us an
understanding, that we may know him that
is true, and we are in him that is true, even
in his Son Jesus Christ. This is the true God,
and eternal life. Little children, keep yourselves from idols. Amen.*

And, then there are of God's children those who have submitted completely to His reign. They are the ones who have come to truly understand God's love, having surrendered by denying self, sin, and satan, who trust God, and are overcomers, living victorious lives! Romans 3:23 says:

> *For all have sinned, and come short of the glory of God.*

True, but the Bible does not teach us to remain in our sins, or it does not teach that we will not sin. It teaches us to not willfully sin, and,

> *If we confess our sins, he is faithful and just to forgive us our sins, and to cleanse us from all unrighteousness. If we say that we have not sinned, we make him a liar, and his word is not in us* **(1 John 1:9-10).**

If we say we are saved, and are walking in sin without any conviction, of the Holy Spirit, we deceive ourselves! 1 John 2:18-19 takes us further by saying:

> *Little children, it is the last time: and as ye have heard that antichrist shall come, even now are there many antichrists; whereby we know that it is the last time* **[or last days].** *They went out from us, but they were not of us; for if they had been of us, they would no doubt have continued with us: but they went out, that they might be made manifest that they were not all of us."*

What John is simply saying is that there were some who followed Jesus, but were not saved in the beginning. So now they are in the world, professing to be saved, but actually are (directly opposite to) against Christ. Jesus said Himself:

He that is not with me is against me; and he that gathereth not with me scattereth abroad (Matthew 12:30).

As servants of God's kingdom, He is responsible for our welfare, protection, and justice. So when Jesus began to teach kingdom living, He said,

No man can serve two masters: for either he will hate the one, and love the other; or else he will hold to the one, and despise the other. Ye cannot serve God and mammon (Matthew 6:24).

We either trust God, or we trust another or ourselves. When we truly surrender to the will of God, evidence is shown in that we no longer allow carnality in our thinking. We intentionally have laid aside every weight and the sin that so easily beset us. In other words, we overcame our sins with the help of prayer, fasting, and the empowerment of the Holy Ghost. We have put our confidence completely in God, and no longer are we fearful, nor worried. Why? Christ is living through us. Christ is forming in us as we are continuing to grow spiritually mature (Hebrews 12:1; 1 John 5:14-15; Galatians 4:19).

Paul tells us in Philippians 4:6-7,

Be careful **[anxious]** *for nothing; but in every thing by prayer and supplication with thanksgiving let your requests be made known unto God. And the peace of God, which passeth all understanding, shall keep* **[guard]** *your hearts and minds through Christ Jesus.*

Section I - Get Wisdom; Get Understanding

In the sixth chapter of the gospel of Matthew, Jesus teaches us to take no thought to physical substance, that God will supply our every need. He explains about how God provides for the fowls of the air, the lilies, and grass of the fields, and that we are just as important to Him as they are. He explains that when we take thought to what we will drink, eat, and with what we are to be clothed in. We only have little faith. Our faith increases as we continue trusting God.

Within the kingdom of God, we are under His watchful eye, as with all of creation. We are in the secret place of the Most High, abiding in Him because of our trust. God's protection upon us is divinely provided. We have a special connection with God. The psalmist speaks of God's protection as a refuge and a fortress. His angels are given charge over us. Psalm 91:1-11 says:

> *He that dwelleth in the secret place of the most High shall abide under the shadow of the Almighty. I will say of the LORD, He is my refuge and my fortress: my God; in him will I trust. Surely he shall deliver thee from the snare of the fowler, and from the noisome pestilence. He shall cover thee with his feathers, and under his wings shalt thou trust: his truth shall be thy shield and buckler. Thou shalt not be afraid for the terror by night; nor for the arrow that flieth by day; Nor for the pestilence that walketh in darkness; nor for the destruction that wasteth at noonday. A thousand shall fall at thy side, and ten thousand at thy right hand; but it shall not come nigh thee. Only with thine eyes shalt thou behold and see the reward of the wicked. Because thou hast made the LORD, which is my refuge, even*

*the most High, thy habitation; There shall
no evil befall thee, neither shall any plague
come nigh thy dwelling. For he shall give
his angels charge over thee, to keep thee in
all thy ways.*

The Bible tells us that our God stands for Justice. He is a Just God. The psalmist says in Psalm 82:1-5, 7-8:

*God standeth in the congregation of the
mighty; he judgeth among the gods. How
long will ye judge unjustly, and accept the
persons of the wicked? Selah. Defend the
poor and fatherless: do justice to the afflict
ed and needy. Deliver the poor and needy:
rid them out of the hand of the wicked. They
know not, neither will they understand; they
walk on in darkness: all the foundations of
the earth are out of course ... I have said, Ye
are gods; and all of you are children of the
most High. But ye shall die like men, and fall
like one of the princes. Arise, O God, judge
the earth: for thou shalt inherit all nations.*

God has ordained earthly judges to represent him on earth. The word gods represents judges who were unjustly representing God, and this psalm is concerning problems with these unjust judges who were not representing God's people fairly.

The psalmist Asaph is seeking God's judgment upon the entire earth, and these unjust judges, because of their wickedness. We must understand that God is the Supreme Judge over all nations, and people. We can seek God to vindicate any wrongs to which we are subjected. Psalm 97:1, 9-12 says:

Section I - Get Wisdom; Get Understanding

THE LORD reigneth; let the earth rejoice;
let the multitude of isles be glad thereof. For
thou, LORD, art high above all the earth:
thou art exalted far above all gods. Ye that
love the LORD, hate evil: he preserveth the
souls of his saints; he delivereth them out of
the hand of the wicked. Light is sown for
the righteous, and gladness for the upright
in heart. Rejoice in the LORD, ye righteous;
and give thanks at the remembrance of his
holiness.

He is above all things, and answers to no one!

We must discipline ourselves in giving, prayer and fasting. It is how we trust, communicate, and fellowship or commune with God. All three are learned behaviors. It is through giving that we exercise our faith. Giving is an expression of love. It is through prayer that we receive strength, and the power of God. It is through fasting that we humble our souls. Practical applications of God's word empowers us, and obtaining knowledge about who God is, his power and authority is what enables us to trust Him. He is above all things, and answers to nobody. His presence is everywhere, and He is all-powerful. Truly knowing and understanding God is what gives us confidence in Him.

Therefore, we must first seek His righteousness. We must seek to understand all that is provided for us in His kingdom. And, as we seek God, He says,

all these things shall be added unto you
(Matthew 6:33c).

Imagine spending quality time studying God's word, praying, and fasting. Spending sincere time in worship and praise. Spending quality time in fellowship with the saints,

26

as we seek the kingdom of God, and His righteousness. We are working together to build the kingdom of God in our service to the Lord in whatever profession, career, or vocation to which we apply our gifts and talents.

The challenge to us is obedience. Are we going to obey God's Word? When we truly seek to understand God, and what Jesus' death on the cross really means, we will no longer have a problem trusting Him!

✝

—2—

The Economy of God

The earth is the Lord's, and the fullness thereof;
The world, and they that dwell therein
(Psalm 24:1).

The United States of America has an economy. Likewise, the economy of God is the economy that not only provides resources for the people of God, but for every living creature on the earth. Psalm 24:1 says:

> *The earth is the LORD's and the fullness*
> *thereof; the world, and they that dwell*
> *therein.*

Paul speaks about the wisdom of God, which the natural neither carnal man can receive, because it is spiritually discerned. Paul says:

> *But we speak the wisdom of God in a mys-*
> *tery, even the hidden wisdom, which God*
> *ordained before the world unto our glory:*
> *Which none of the princes of this world knew:*
> *for had they known it, they would not have*
> *crucified the Lord of glory. But as it is writ*
> *ten, **eye hath not seen, nor ear heard,***
> ***neither have entered into the heart of***
> ***man, the things which God hath pre-***
> ***pared for them that love him.** But God*
> *hath revealed them unto us by his Spirit: for*

28

*the Spirit searcheth all things, yea, the deep
things of God.*

The apostle Paul goes on to say:

> *But the natural man receiveth not the things
> of the Spirit of God: for they are foolish-
> ness unto him: neither can he know them,
> because they are spiritually discerned. But
> he that is spiritual judgeth all things, yet he
> himself is judged of no man.* **For who hath
> known the mind of the Lord, that he
> may instruct him? But we have the
> mind of Christ.** *And I, brethren, could not
> speak unto you as unto spiritual, but as unto
> carnal, even as unto babes in Christ. I have
> fed you with milk, and not with meat: for
> hitherto ye were not able to bear it, neither
> yet now are ye able* (1 Corinthians 2:7-10,
> 14-16; 3:1-2).

Therefore, the natural and carnal minded is not able to
discern (see, perceive, and/or understand) spiritual things,
or the spiritual things of God. Our perception will only
change as we renew our minds through the word of God,
and then the Holy Spirit will enlighten the eyes of our understanding, giving us revelation of God's kingdom, His
economy, and the purpose of the law of the tithe. The economy of God includes the earth and all of its forces and ener-
gies. It includes all money can buy and everything that is
produced. Everything comes from the earth and belongs to
the Lord. Included in God's economy are the benefits re
corded that are recorded in Psalm 103. We own nothing.
We own absolutely nothing. Man was given dominion over
the distribution of God's resources.

But man's greed has brought us to this sad state of affairs. The poor are getting poorer, and the rich are getting richer. But, for the citizens of God's kingdom, He disperses from above everything we need, and desire. Paul the apostle says:

> *But my God shall supply all your need according to his riches in glory by Christ Jesus* (Philippians 4:19).

The psalmist goes on to say:

> *For the LORD God is a sun and shield: the LORD will give grace and glory: no good thing will he withhold from them that walk uprightly (Psalm 84:11).*

Jesus then says:

> *Ask, and it shall be given you; seek, and you shall find; knock, and it shall be opened unto you* (Matthew 7:7-8).

We were brought into partnership with God, when He created Adam, assigned him a function, and gave him dominion over all the earth. And ever since then, we were made accountable to God, and what we do with the resources, He has entrusted to us. Every living being belongs to God, for the Bible says,

> *...we were brought with a price, not with silver nor gold, but with the Precious Blood of the Lamb, who was slain before the foundation of the world (Revelation 13:8).*

Ephesians 2:10 says:

> *For we are his workmanship, created in Christ Jesus unto good works, which God hath before ordained that we should walk in them.*

Then, 1 Corinthians 3:9 goes on to say that we are co-laborers together with God in the building of His kingdom. Therefore, we are His partners. The partnership agreement made by God says, He gets the first tenth, and we are given the other nine tenths. We are allowed to work as His partners on earth earning a wage while we labor to build the kingdom of God, in whatever vocation, occupation, career or profession we, through the direction of God, have chosen.

In the partnership agreement, the tithe belongs to God. It is a spiritual mark of God. It is the visible sign of our trust in Him. Again, Malachi 3:8 says:

> *Will a man rob God? Yet ye have robbed me.*
> *But ye say, Wherein have we robbed thee?*
> *In tithes and offerings.*

So, the tithe indicates that the offerings came before the tithing system. We see the first sacrifice in Genesis 3:21, and the first offering in Genesis 4:4, which says:

> *And in the process of time it came to pass, that Cain brought of the fruit of the ground an offering unto the LORD. And Abel, he also brought of the firstlings of his flock and of the fat thereof. And the LORD had respect unto Abel and to his offering.*

The second offering shown in scripture is in Genesis 8:20, which says:

> *And Noah builded an altar unto the LORD; and took of every clean beast, and of every clean fowl, and offered burnt offerings on the altar.*

Now, the first record of the tithe is found in Genesis 14:18-20, and it says:

> *And Melchizedek king of Salem brought forth bread and wine: and he was the priest of the most high God. And he blessed him, and said, Blessed be Abram of the most high God, possessor of heaven and earth: And blessed be the most high God, which hath delivered thine enemies into thy hand. And he gave him tithes of all.*

The second account of the tithe is recorded in Genesis 28:22, when Jacob vowed to give the tithe of all God blessed him with.

Notice, this is before the Law was given to Moses. The Bible says:

> *And Jacob vowed a vow, saying, If God will be with me, and will keep me in this way that I go, and will give me bread to eat, and raiment to put on, So that I come again to my father's house in peace; then shall the LORD be my God: And this stone, which I have set for a pillar, shall be God's house: and of all that thou shalt give me I will surely give the tenth unto thee* (Genesis 28:20-22).

Jacob recognized God as the source of His protection, providence, and partnership. As partners of God, we are given the ability to prosper. Deuteronomy 8:18 says:

> *But thou shalt remember the LORD thy God: for it is he that giveth thee power to get wealth, that he may establish his covenant which he sware unto thy fathers, as it is this day.*

Our success is in God, and not by the world's standard. We must not be slothful, but diligent in the things God purposed in our lives. In the parable of the talents, Jesus is the man who traveled to a far country. Before leaving He gave his three servants talents according to their abilities. He gave to one five talents, and to another two, and to the last one. Well, the servant He gave five talents, increased his to ten. The servant He gave two talents, increase his to four. But, the servant He gave one talent took his and buried it in the ground. When the master returned He saw that the two servants who were given the five and two talents had doubled them.

He said to the both,

> *Well done, thou good and faithful servant: thou hast been faithful over a few things, I will make thee ruler over many things: enter thou into the joy of thy Lord.* (Matthew 25:21)

But, to the servant who had buried his talent in the ground.

> *His Lord answered and said unto him, Thou wicked and slothful, servant, thou knewest that I reap where I sowed not, and gather where I have not strawed* **[spread the grain***]: Thou oughtest therefore to have put my money to the exchangers, and then at my coming I should have received mine own with usury* **[interest]** (Matthew 25:26-27).

The one talent was taken from the wicked and slothful servant, and given to the servant that had ten talents. Jesus then commanded that the wicked and slothful servant be cast into outer darkness.

Section I - Get Wisdom; Get Understanding

The wicked and slothful servant was cast into outer darkness, because he was not a true servant of the master. He did not know the Lord, had he known the master. He would have known that the Lord is merciful, and kind. His response to the master was,

> *And I was afraid, and went and hid thy talent in the earth: lo, there thou hast is thine* (Matthew 25:25).

The master wanted to show the servants one, his generosity, and two, he wanted them to experience the joy of faithful service. The wicked and slothful servant did not personally know, nor serve the Lord. Remember, we are talking about working as a partner with God, building the kingdom. So you and I must understand that whatever talent or gift given to us, we must not be slothful. We must use our talents and gifts in the faithful service of the Lord.

The wicked and slothful servant was fearful. Fear will paralyze us, but walking in the truth paralyzes the enemy.

The first revelation of walking in the truth of God's word came when I was convoying to my first annual training to Grayling, Michigan, in 1986. I was looking forward to the two weeks away from home, because I had planned to fast, and draw closer to God through the study and meditation of the Word. I was unaware at that time of the activities of the spiritual realm, it came later that year. As we travel along the freeway, I noticed road kill. I began to ponder while talking to God about them having eyes yet not seeing. God spoke and said, When they see the light, it paralyzes them, and they are struck.

When the enemy see the light, as the results of us walking in the truth of God's Word, it paralyzes him. The only foothold he has in the believer's life is sin. Jesus was without sin, and He said to His disciples in John 14:30, *"Hereafter I will not talk much with you: for the prince of this world cometh, and hath nothing in me."* Sin or darkness is satan's domain, and his evil forces has a legal right to dwell there. Therefore, John the apostle tells us in (1 John 5:18-19) that: *"We know that whosoever is born of God sinneth not; But he that is begotton of God keepeth himself, and that Wicked one toucheth him not. And we know that we are of God, and the whole world lieth in wickedness, or (darkness)."* So we must understand that fear is not of God. The apostle Paul told Timothy:

> *...stir up the gift of God, which is in thee by the putting on of my hands. For God hath not given us the spirit of fear; but of power, and love, and of a sound mind. Be not thou therefore ashamed of the testimony of our Lord, nor of me his prisoner: but be thou partaker of the afflictions of the gospel according to the power of God; Who hath saved us, and called us with an holy calling, not according to our works, but according to his own purpose and grace, which was given us in Christ Jesus before the world began, But is now made manifest by the appearing of our Savior Jesus Christ, who hath abolished death, and hath brought life and immortality to light through the gospel* (2 Timothy 1:6-10).

God has given to the true believer the spirit of power, the spirit of love, and the spirit of a sound mind. We use the spirit of power to overcome self, sin, and satan. It also is used in the work of the ministry and to prosper us. The spirit of love enables us to love God, one another, and the world. The spirit of a sound mind enables us to make right decisions. Therefore scripture says:

Whosoever shall confess that Jesus is the Son of God, God dwelleth in him, and he is in God. And we have known and believed the love that God hath to us. God is love; and he that dwelleth in love dwelleth in God, and God in him. Herein is our love made [mature] perfect, that we may have boldness in the day of judgment: because as he is, so are we in this world. There is no fear in love; but [mature] perfect love casteth out fear: because fear hath torment. He that feareth is not made [mature] perfect in love (1 John 4:15-18).

The kingdom of God is the body of Christ, which is the present-day church. Christ is the head of the body, or church. The church is the work of God's ministry in the earth. We are told in Ephesians 4:4-7 that:

There is one body, and one Spirit, even as ye are called in one hope of your calling; One Lord, one faith, one baptism, One God and Father of all, who is above all, and through all, and in you all. But unto every one of us is given grace according to the measure of the gift of Christ.

We all have been given faith to exercise the gifts given to us by Christ. In order to exercise our gifts we must have faith. God has given to every man a measure of faith (Romans 12:3).

What we do with our faith is a different story. Jesus tells us to have faith in God (Mark 11:22). We could not have been saved without faith, and without faith it is impossible to please God. The apostle Paul goes on to share with us, that before Jesus ascended to God, He first descended into the lower parts of the earth, where He led captivity captive, and gave gifts unto men. Jesus then ascended up far above all heavens, to where God sits, that He might fill or fulfill all things. Jesus is sitting on the right hand of the throne of God. Before Jesus ascended to God, Paul tells us that He gave the church gifts, for the equipping of the saints, for the work of God's ministry on earth.

> *And he gave some, apostles; and some, prophets; and some evangelists; and some, pastors and teachers; For the perfecting of the saints, for the work of the ministry, for the edifying of the body of Christ: Till we all come in the unity of the faith, and of the knowledge of the Son of God, unto a perfect man, unto the measure of the stature of the fullness of Christ* (Ephesians 4:11-13).

Jesus gave gifts to the church to edify the body. In other words, for us to be nurtured so as to grow spiritually mature, to form us into the image of Christ so that we will not be children carried about with every wind of doctrine or teaching of men, in whom the false prophets and teachers are waiting to deceive us. We are to speak the truth in love, speaking of the gifts given to the church, so that the saints may grow up into Him in all areas of life, which is in Christ, the head. Paul now makes known that the church's growth is the result of the edifying of love. The apostle Paul says:

> *From whom the whole body fitly joined to gether and compacted by that which every joint supplieth according to the effectual working in the measure of every part, maketh increase of the body unto the edifying of itself in love* (Ephesians 4:16).

Paul says that the growth of the church increases as the saints are edified in love, and as every member learns to

37

function within the gifts to which they have been given. For we are of one body, but many members, and we all have not the same function, or gifts. But, that the same Spirit works in us, to the edifying of the body, so we must individually seek God's purpose and plans for our lives, and in the process, we are to be renewed in the spirit of our minds, and we are to put on the new man, which is created after God in righteousness and true holiness. Paul is saying for us to walk, and live in the spirit, which is our new nature, while exercising our faith in God, and for us to grow spiritually mature.

Therefore, the work of the Lord is a service of Love. We work as laborers of God, working together to build the kingdom. We are God's instruments of righteousness. It is the expressed love of Jesus Christ that we show to others in the attempt to draw them to God (Romans 6:12-13). Scripture says that If we do not love our brother, who we have seen, who then can say they love God, in whom they have not seen.

> *We love him, because he first loved us. If a man say, I love God, and hateth his brother, he is a liar: for he that loveth not his brother whom he hath seen, how can he love God whom he hath not seen? And this commandment have we from him, That he who loveth God love his brother also* (1 John 4:19-21).

Loving God, and one another honors Him! Proverbs 3:7-10 says:

> *Be not wise in thine own eyes: fear the LORD, and depart from evil. It shall be health to thy navel, and marrow to thy bones. Honour the LORD with thy substance, and with the firstfruits of all thine increase: So shall thy barns be filled with plenty, and thy presses*

2- The Economy of God

shall burst out with new wine.

We are God's workmanship, entrusted with the resource of God, therefore we should honor Him. The tithe honors God. Many say, "I honor, I praise, and I magnify your name. But won't give God the tithe, because of unbelief.

Wisdom says: "All wages that we receive (accumulate) contribute to our bottom line." Wise money management gives us two choices. One, we can learn to save. Or two, we can learn to invest. However instead of making wise choices we end up spending our money foolishly. Women, for example, buy shoes, and already have thirty pairs. Wisdom says, "use what you have, buy the dress for the shoes, and not the shoes for the dress." Men may throw their hard earned money away on gambling or the lottery, rather than build a nest egg, for their families. Our financial problems exist because we are not tithing, and some who are tithing do not know how to (live within one's means) manage their money wisely!

✟

—3—

Understanding the Tithe

...Render to Caesar the things that are Caesar's,
and to God the things that are God's. And they
marvelled at him (Mark 12:17).

The tithe belongs to God and is a spiritual mark of God. The visible sign that we trust Him. God established the tithing system for the purpose of financing the work of ministry on the earth, and to teach man the fear of the LORD (Deuteronomy 14:22-29). Many now say that tithing was under the law, and we are now under grace, or that tithing was for the Jews of the past and that the tithe is part of the ceremonial system introduced by the old covenant law of Moses. No! The law of the tithe is now in effect, to this day.

The tithing system was established before the law. Scripture says in Hebrews 7:1-10:

> *For this Melchisedec, king of Salem, priest*
> *of the most high God, who met Abraham re-*
> *turning from the slaughter of the kings, and*
> *blessed him; To whom also Abraham gave*
> *a tenth part of all; first being by interpre*
> *tation King of righteousness, and after that*
> *also King of Salem, which is, King of peace;*
> *Without father, without mother, without*
> *descent, having neither beginning of days,*
> *nor end of life; but made like unto the Son of*
> *God; abideth a priest continually. Now con-*
> *sider how great this man was, unto whom*
> *the patriarch Abraham gave the tenth of*
> *the spoils. And verily they that are of the*

> sons of Levi, **who receive the office of
> the priesthood**, have a commandment
> **[by Moses]** to take tithes of the people ac-
> cording to the law, that is, of their brethren,
> though they come out of the loins of Abra-
> ham: But he whose descent is not counted
> from them received tithes of Abraham, and
> blessed him that had the promises. And
> without all contradiction the less is blessed
> of the better. And here men that die receive
> tithes; but there he receiveth them, of whom
> it is witnessed that he liveth. And as I may
> so say, Levi also, who receiveth tithes, paid
> tithes in Abraham. For he was yet in the
> loins of his father, when Melchisedec met
> him.

The tithing system was under the priesthood of
Melchizedek. Melchizedek was a higher rank (than the
Levitical priesthood) Jesus Christ holding the same rank,
(spiritual and divine) than of the Levitical priesthood (who
were mere human and fleshly) established during Moses'
time. Scripture goes on to say:

> If therefore perfection were by the Levitical
> priesthood, (for under it the people received
> the law,) what further need was there that
> another priest should rise after the order
> of Melchisedec, and not be called after the
> order of Aaron? For the priesthood being
> changed, there is made of necessity a change
> also of the law. **[The law changed from
> the natural to spiritual]** For he of whom
> these things are spoken pertaineth to anoth-
> er tribe, of which no man gave attendance
> at the altar. For it is evident that our Lord

41

sprang out of Judah; of which tribe Moses spake nothing concerning priesthood. And it is yet far more evident: for that after the similitude of Melchisedec there ariseth another priest, Who is made, not after the law of a carnal commandment, but after the power of an endless life. For he testifieth,•Thou art a priest for ever after the order of Melchisedec. (Hebrews 7:11-17).

Let's understand what this passage of scriptures is saying. These vital scriptures begin to compare the two priesthoods. Notice back in patriarchal times, TITHING was God's system for financing His ministry. Melchizedek was High Priest. The patriarch Abraham, it's written, knew and kept God's commandments, His statutes and laws (Genesis 26:5). And he (Abraham) paid tithes to the High Priest!

Then, the statement is made in this passage that during that dispensation from Moses until Christ, the priests of that time —the Levites— took tithes from the people by law of the tithe. It was a law started in the beginning, and continued through the Mosaic dispensation. Tithing then, did not begin with Moses! The old covenant is gone, that's true. But its ending could not take away what it did not bring! Tithing was God's law hundreds of years before the old covenant started. Therefore, the tithing system is a law established by the Law Maker for the purpose of financing the ministry or work of God in the earth. We can compare another law established by God—marriage, and man is trying to change it by man's law. Same-sex marriages are an abomination to God. Once God establishes a law, man cannot change it because he does not want to comply. Whether we want to accept it or not, tithing is a law. The Lord inclined my ear saying, man cannot change the law of gravity, neither can he change the law of the tithe. Unbelief does not nullify the word of God.

Scripture shows that the tithe was presented to God at places of worship (Genesis 14:17-24; 28:20-22). Through-out the Bible we see the alter, the tabernacle, the synagogue, the temple, and now the church. God establish the tithing system for the purpose of maintaining His place of worship on earth, and to teach man to walk upright (Proverbs 16:6).

> *to teach man the fear of the LORD.*

God in His infinite wisdom knew it was not in man's self ish heart to give. So He commanded the blessings through obedience, because of the disobedience of Adam to obey the personal commandment of God not to eat of the tree of the knowledge of good and evil. All of mankind was cursed. God is still saying to us to choose life or death, to choose blessings or curses. Why? Because we still have free will (Genesis 3; Deuteronomy 28).

God in His infinite wisdom knew that we all could afford to pay the tithe. It is only a matter of our faith, obedience, trust, and living wisely. When you really think about it, ten cents from a dollar is not very much to give God, and we can easily live off the other ninety cent, if we live wisely.

In God's fairness, it does not matter how much our gross incomes are; we all are paying the same according to God. Let's look at things from a worldly perspective. In Mark 12:13-17, Jesus was questioned about the tribute (tax) to Caesar, by,

> *...certain of the Pharisees and of the Herodi-ans, to catch him in his words. And when they were come, they say unto him, Master, we know that thou art true, and carest for no man: for thou regardest not the person of men, but teachest the way of God in truth: Is it lawful to give tribute to Ceasar, or not? Shall we give, or shall we not give? But he*

43

knowing their hypocrisy, said unto them, Why tempt ye me? Bring me a penny, that I may see it. And they brought it. And he saith unto them. Whose is this image and super-scription? And they said unto him, Caesar's. And Jesus answering said unto them, Ren-der to Caesar the things that are Caesar's, and to God the things that are God's. And they marveled at him (Mark 12:13-17).

We, like the Pharisees and Herodians, should not be sur-prised by God's law of the tithe. It is the visible sign that we trust in God. Think about this: what else do we have to ren-der to God? We own nothing, absolutely nothing. But we are to give God praise, honor, and glory, because it belongs to Him. There are also two extremes. For example, right and wrong, up and down, good and bad. Likewise, there are tithes and taxes. The tithe is the other side of the coin when it comes to the spiritual realm of God's kingdom. It is the resource used for the purpose of financing God's ministry here on earth. It is within the economy of God that we pay our tithes to the church.

Another issue we should deal with is using God's house of prayer as a house of merchandise. Prior to the account of the tribute, Jesus had cleansed the temple of those who were making merchandise of the house of God. It says;

*Jesus went into the temple, and began to cast out them that sold and bought in the temple, and overthrew the tables of the moneychangers, and the seats of them that sold doves; And would not suffer that any man should carry any vessel [is] (merchan-dise) [is] through the temple. And he taught, saying unto them, **is it not written, my house shall be called of all nations the***

house of prayer? But ye have made it a
den of thieves. And the scribes and chief
priests heard it, and sought how they might
destroy him: for they feared him, because
all the people was astonished at his doctrine
(Mark 11:15-18).

When Jesus cleansed the temple, He was only enforc-
ing the laws already in place to prevent the misuse of God's
house. Jesus no longer wants to see clothing hung in front,
or along side some churches. He no longer wants to see barbecue and fish fry signs posted outside some of our churches.
He no longer wants to see friendly seeker churches manipu-
lating the world and His people, but preaching and teaching
the kingdom of God. When the church obeys the law of the
tithe, we will be able to finance God's ministry without the
use of these things.

The offerings given to the church, on the other hand, are
to be used to help the poor and needy. One thing I have
learned in ministry is that we must have compassion. Jesus
had compassion on the multitude. He not only met their
spiritual needs, but He also met the physical needs of the
people, by feeding them after being taught, and coming from
afar (Matthew 9:35-38; Matthew 14:14-21). We too must
have compassion on those to whom we minister the word.
We must assess the need of each individual, and help resolve
that need. Whatever we see that is hindering that individual
from receiving the Word of God, it may be employment, the
need of decent housing, or just having food and clothing for
their bodies—we are to be open to help them.

The economy of God is the stewardship over the resources of God, and we must use them wisely. All that is in
the earth belongs to the Lord. So whatever we have of the
Lord should be to His disposal, if in fact we are His children.

We need the wisdom of God to determine a real need, so as not to be deceived or used by those we witness to, or minister the word.

The purpose of Proverbs is for us to know wisdom and instruction, and to discern the words of understanding. To have the ability to distinguish between what is true and what is false, what is right and what is wrong. Solomon said:

> *For the LORD giveth wisdom: out of his mouth cometh knowledge and understanding. He layeth up sound wisdom for the righteous: he is a buckler to them that walk uprightly. He keepeth the paths of judgment, and preserveth the way of his saints. Then shalt thou understand righteousness, and judgment, and equity; yea, every good path. When wisdom entereth into thine heart, and knowledge is pleasant unto thy soul; Discretion shall preserve thee, understanding shall keep thee: To deliver thee from the way of the evil man, from the man that speaketh froward things* (Proverbs 2:6-12).

We must ask for God's wisdom through prayer, and He will give us knowledge and understanding. This takes us to John 15:7-16. Jesus tells His disciples that they did not choose Him, but that He chose and ordained them, that they should go and bring forth fruit, and that their fruit should remain, and that whatsoever they shall ask of the Father in His name, the Father would give it to them for herein was His Father glorified. The condition of this promise was that they were to abide in Him, and His word was to abide in them. Also, they were to love one another as the Father has loved Him, and as He has loved them, and they were commanded to continue in His love.

46

Continuing in obedience of the word produces the fruit of the Spirit, and the by-product of Jesus' love is joy. Therefore, Jesus said:

> *These things have I spoken unto you, that my joy might remain in you, and that your joy might be full. This is my commandment, That ye love one another, as I have loved you. Greater love hath no man than this, that a man lay down his life for his friends. Ye are my friends, if ye do whatsoever I command you (John 15:11-14).*

Giving the tithe honors God, and when we love and trust God we will obey the law of the tithe, because it develops consistency. When we surrender our will to God, in obedience, we will grow mature, spiritually!

✝

Section II

Becoming Financially Successful

—4—

Wisdom Defined

For the Lord giveth wisdom: out of his mouth cometh knowledge and understanding
(Proverbs 2:6).

Wisdom is a gift. It is an accurate perception into the nature of things, and having knowledge alone is not wisdom; you must apply knowledge skillfully to have wisdom, or to become wise.

Wisdom is the God-given ability or power to apply knowledge skillfully in all aspects of life. Therefore, wisdom is the practical application of God's Word to one's life. It is what makes us wise. Wisdom basically means skill in living, or it refers to the skill to live life successfully. It also includes physical, and artistic skills. The key to becoming wise is to depart from evil, and to seek God. Proverbs 3:7-8,13 says: *"Be not wise in thine own eyes: fear the LORD, and depart from evil. It shall be health to thy navel, and marrow to thy bones. Happy is the man that findeth wis dom, and the man that getteth understanding."* Again, in the book of Proverbs, it says,

> **The fear of the LORD is the beginning of knowledge:** *but fools despise wisdom* **[the ability to apply knowledge]** *and instruction. If thou seekest her as silver, and searchest for her as for hid treasures: Then shalt thou understand the fear of the LORD, and find the knowledge of God. For the LORD giveth wisdom: out of his mouth cometh knowledge and understanding* (Proverbs 1:7, 2:4-6).

50

Wisdom says:

> *By mercy and truth iniquity is purged: and*
> *by the fear of the LORD men depart from*
> *evil* (Proverbs 16:6).

The fear of the LORD is to walk upright, or to walk in obedience to God. Proverbs 14:2 confirms this by saying:

> *He that walketh in his uprightness feareth*
> *the LORD: but he that is perverse in his*
> *ways despiseth (rejects) him.*

Jesus knowing says:

> *No man can serve two masters: for either*
> *he will hate the one, and love the other; or*
> *else he will hold to the one, and despise the*
> *other. Ye cannot serve God and mammon*
> **[or wealth]** (Matthew 6:24).

One example of wisdom is knowledge applied skillfully to reveal something. As with the story of the two harlots who were living together, and each had a child. During the night one of them laid on her child and the child died. They both came before Solomon, each claiming that the living child belonged to her. The woman whose child was alive spoke the narrative of what had happened. After going back and forth as to whom the living child belonged Solomon said:

> *Bring me a sword. And they brought a*
> *sword before the king. And the king said,*
> *Divide the living child in two, and give half*
> *to the one, and half to the other. Then spake*
> *the woman whose the living child was unto*
> *the king, for her bowels yearned upon her*

*son, and she said, O my lord, give her the
living child, and in no wise slay it. But the
other said, Let it be neither mine nor thine,
but divide it. Then the king answered and
said, Give her* **[the one that yearned
upon her son]** *the living child, and in no
wise slay it: she is the mother thereof. And
all Israel heard of the judgment which the
king had judged; and they feared the king:
for they saw that the wisdom of God was in
him, to do judgment* (1 Kings 3:25-28).

Judgment means the ability to make a wise decision.
Solomon had no other way of telling who the child's mother
was, except by the answer given.

The gift of discernment and wisdom go hand in hand. It
is not judging by what appears to be, but knowing as the result of God's Spirit or accumulated learning, which is knowledge. The spiritual realm is just as real as the physical or
natural world. The gift of discernment is the gift given to us
to discern spiritual things, or the spiritual thing of God. In
our natural ability, we are able to discern to a degree, but
the gift of discernment goes beyond our physical senses. We
connect with God, and the Holy Spirit reveals to us whatever
we need to know, when we need to know it.

Proverbs 1:5-7 says:

*A wise man will hear, and will increase
learning; and a man of understanding shall
attain unto wise counsels:*

It goes on to say:

*To understand a proverb, and the interpre-
tation; the words of the wise, and their dark
sayings. The fear of the LORD is the begin-*

ning of knowledge: but fools despise wisdom
and instruction.

God gives us the ability to use knowledge skillfully in
life. The simplicity of this story is that the child's mother
would rather see someone else with her child, then for her
child to die.

God is our source of wisdom. So, James 1:5-8 says:

> If any of you lack wisdom, let him ask of
> God, that giveth to all men liberally, and
> upbraideth **[hold back]** not; and it shall
> be given him. But let him ask in faith, noth-
> ing wavering. For he that wavereth is like
> a wave of the sea driven with the wind and
> tossed. For let not that man think that he
> shall receive any thing of the Lord. A double
> minded man is unstable in all his ways.

James the apostle is referring to a double-minded man
as one who is trying to live for God, and live in the world at
the same time. James says this man is unstable in all his
ways. We find stability in God, because we cannot serve two
masters. I recommend reading the book of Proverbs every
month, a chapter a day. Read the last two chapters together
when there are thirty days in a month.. You will be truly
blessed of God.

The knowledge that will make us wise is found in God's
word, which is truth, and truth is absolute, which means
perfect, having no defects or fault: flawless; accurate, abso
lute. Psalm 119:105 tells us:

> Thy word is a lamp unto my feet, and a light
> unto my path.

Jesus also said in John 14:6-7;

> *I am the way, the truth, and the life: no man*
> *cometh unto the Father, but by me. If ye had*
> *known me, ye should have known my Father*
> *also, and from henceforth ye know him, and*
> *have seen him.*

We know that Jesus is the manifestation of the word, so the scripture says:

> *In the beginning was the Word, and the*
> *Word was with God, and the Word was God.*
> *The same was in the beginning with God.*
> *All things were made by him; and without*
> *him was not any thing made that was made.*
> *In him was life; and the life was the light of*
> *men. And the light shineth in darkness; and*
> *the darkness comprehended it not.*

Scripture goes on to say:

> *And the Word was made flesh, and dwelt*
> *among us, (and we beheld his glory, the glo-*
> *ry as of the only begotten of the Father,) full*
> *of grace and truth.* (John 1:1-5; 14).

Jesus is the word of God!

We must seek the truth of God's Word concerning the financial aspects of our lives, which is found in God's word, and then apply it to our finances. We then will become skill ful, or wise financially. Wealth accumulated deceitfully, will cause us to become unfruitful. (Matthew 13:22). We must be a doers of the Word, and not hearers only!
John 8:31-32 says:

4 Wisdom Defined

*Then said Jesus to those Jews which believed
on him, If ye continue in my word, then are
ye my disciples indeed; And ye shall know
the truth, and the truth shall make you free.*

The truth of God's word makes us free from sin (salvation), bondage (debt), fear, worry, anxiety, and the cares of this world. Read Philippians 4:6-7; 11, 19.

God's knowledge teaches us how to live in every aspect of life, and the wisdom of God, which is God's cleverness, teaches us how to apply that knowledge. Clever is defined as mentally quick, showing dexterity and skill, cleverness. God gives us the ability to apply knowledge skillfully, which enables us to understand our true needs, and then pursue those needs, rather than pursuing covetousness. Covetousness is deceitful, and is a spirit of deception. It looks only at the immediate gratification of what is desired or wanted. It was one of the sins that caused Lucifer to rebel against God; the other sin was pride. Covetousness causes a person to become unthankful and ungrateful of what one already possesses in life.

Covetousness is the by-product of discontentment, whereas joy is the by-product of love. Contentment is the other side of the coin of discontentment. To be content is to be satisfied, or the satisfaction of mind without disquiet, a resting of the mind, to accept one's lot in life, while pursuing the things which will bring true happiness. Covetousness is nothing more than craving or longing for what others have, that we do not have, but want. So we strive to get what others have by any means necessary, and yet continue to be dissatisfied, because we feel we deserve more. Jesus' response to a man asking Him to speak to his older brother, to divide the inheritance with him was,

*And he said unto him, Man, who made me a
judge or a divider over you?* (Luke 12:14)

55

And speaking to a crowd to whom the man was among said:

> *Take heed, and beware of covetousness: for a man's life consisteth not in the abundance of the things which he possesseth* (Luke 12:15).

Then Jesus goes on to speak a parable about a certain rich man who, having plenty, and rather than give out of his abundance to the poor, he built bigger barns to store his goods because he was not satisfied, nor grateful, but wanted more. He was rich materially, but poor in the spiritual things of God. God called him a fool, and said that this night his soul was required of him (Luke 12:14-21).

Jesus explains that we too would be foolish like this man, if we accumulate treasure here on earth, only to die and leave it on earth. It is all about giving to one another God's love, and sharing the resources given to us by God. It's all about becoming the righteousness of God, and expressing the love we have received from Him, to others in not only words, but in deeds. God wants you and me to understand that it is not about us, but it is about Him. It is about us glorifying Him. We glorify God by the lives we live. By demonstrating the word being made alive in us. Allowing Christ to reign in our heart, and glorifying God in our bodies, and spirit.

The apostle Paul says in 1 Corinthians 6:20,

> *What? Know ye not that your body is the temple of the Holy Ghost which is in you, which ye have of God, and ye are not your own? For ye are bought with a price: therefore glorify God in your body, and in your spirit, which are God's.*

He wants us, after receiving Christ as our savior, to gain

56

knowledge of His word, to grow and become wise, and to no longer live foolish lives as we did in our former life. We are to desire the things of God, and this will only come out of a love for God. This takes us back to the first commandment which says:

> Love the Lord thy God with all thy heart, and with all thy soul, and with all thy mind (Matthew 22:37).

We must learn to live by faith, and not by sight. We must understand that faith cannot work without love (Romans 1:17).

Therefore the apostle Paul tells us in Galatians 5:1-8;

> **Stand** fast therefore in the liberty where- with Christ hath made us free, and be not entangled again with the yoke of bondage. For we through the Spirit wait for the hope of righteousness by faith. For in Jesus Christ neither circumcision availeth any thing, nor uncircumcision; but faith which worketh by love. Ye did run well; who did hinder you that ye should not obey the truth? This per- suasion cometh not of him that calleth you.

This persuasion comes from the god of this world, the spirit of error, the antichrist, the father of lies, who does ev- erything to keep us from acknowledging, and surrendering our will to God.

We demonstrate our love for God by giving our lives to Him (Romans 12:1-2). It is an act of our will that we surren- der to God. When we receive Christ in our hearts by faith, through grace, we are born of God's Spirit, and must grow in the grace and knowledge of our Lord, Jesus Christ. Wa- ter baptism does not save us. It is an outward sign of an inward change. However, when we are born of God's Spirit, scripture says we are baptized into the body of Christ, and are born-again.

> *But the scripture hath concluded all under sin, that the promise by faith of Jesus Christ might be given to them that believe. But before faith came, we were kept under the law, shut up unto the faith which should afterwards be revealed. Wherefore the law was our schoolmaster to bring us unto Christ, that we might be justified by faith. But after that faith is come, we are no longer under a school master. For ye are all the children of God by faith in Christ Jesus. For as many of you as have been baptized into Christ have put on Christ. There is neither Jew nor Greek, there is neither bond or free, there is neither male nor female: for ye are all one in Christ Jesus. And if ye be Christ's, then are ye Abraham's seed, and heirs according to the promise* (Galatians 3:22-29).

When we are born of the Spirit of God, evenly there will be evidence of the new birth, as we desire and grow spiritually. Jesus in John 3:8 says:

> *The wind bloweth where it listeth, and thou hearest the sound thereof, but canst not tell whence it cometh, and whither it goeth: so is every one that is born of the Spirit.*

The word listeth, means wishes. The wind blow where it wishes, and the word wish, means to desire or long for something; to command or request, a longing or a desire.

Those who are born of God's Spirit has a longing or desire to know God. God places within us a hunger and thirst after righteousness. So the apostle Paul speaks about the sin in the born-again believer's life saying:

> *Know ye not, that so many of us as were baptized into Jesus Christ were baptized into his death? Therefore we are buried with him by baptism into death: that like as Christ was raised up from the dead by the glory of the Father, even so we also should walk in the newness of life* (Romans 6:3-4).

Along with that, the apostle Paul admonishes us saying:

> ***I beseech*** *you therefore, brethren, by the mercies of God, that ye present your bodies a living sacrifice, holy, acceptable unto God, which is your reasonable service. And be not conformed to this world: but be ye transformed by the renewing of your mind, that ye may prove* **[test]** *what is that good, and acceptable, and perfect, will of God* (Romans 12:1-2).

God allows the testing of our faith. For in so doing, we find God's word to be true.

The apostle Paul told Timothy to:

> *Love not the world, neither the things that are in the world. If any man love the world, the love of the Father is not in him. For all that is in the world, the lust of the flesh, and the lust of the eyes, and the pride of life, is not of the Father, but is of the world. And the world passeth away, and the lust thereof: but he that doeth the will of God abideth forever* (1 John 2:15-17).

What then is the will of God? We obey Him. It was the disobedience of Adam which caused the fall of mankind!

Remember, wisdom is knowledge applied to life skillfully. Wisdom reveals the hidden things of God, which can only be known and understood by the recreated spirit. So Jesus says:

> *Not every one that saith unto me, Lord, Lord, shall enter into the kingdom of heaven; but he that doeth the will of my Father which is in heaven* (Matthew 7:21).

Jesus is speaking of the false teacher, and prophets (preachers) who He calls workers of iniquity, who are doing according to their own will. He also reveals that there will be a separation of the unbelievers among us that Jesus calls the goats. After Jesus tells the parable of the talents in Matthew 25:14-30, in verse 31 −34 he says:

> *When the Son of man shall come in his glory, and all the holy angels with him, then shall he sit upon the throne of his glory: And before him shall be gathered all nations: and he shall separate them one from another, as a shepherd divideth his sheep from the goats: And he shall set the sheep on his right hand, but the goats on the left. Then shall the King say unto them on the right hand, Come, ye blessed of my Father, inherit the kingdom prepared for you from the foundation of the world:*

and in verse 41 He says:

> *also unto them on the left hand, Depart from me, ye cursed, into everlasting fire, prepared for the devil and his angels:*

Jesus pronounces this judgment upon them because they did not the will of the Father. We are called to feed the hungry, to clothe the naked, to visit the sick, and those who are in prison. We know that these things are all part of our service to the Lord, and is a description of true religion (Isaiah 58). You do not have to be a saint to do these things. True, but those who are not Christians are prone to do them with the wrong motives. Jeremiah 17:9-11 says:

> *The heart is deceitful above all things, and desperately wicked: who can know it? I the LORD search the heart, I try [test] the reins [mind], even to give every man according to his ways, and according to the fruit of his doings [deeds]. As the partridge sitteth on eggs, and hatcheth them not; so he that getteth riches, and not by right, shall leave them in the midst of his days, and at his end shall be a fool.*

God reigns in the heart of the born-again believer, and wisdom makes us wise, not foolish!

—5—

Financial Success Defined

The blessing of the Lord, it maketh rich, and he addeth no sorrow with it (Proverbs 10:22).

Financial Success from a Biblical Perspective is trusting God with *(the tithe)* ten percent of your gross income, whether weekly, bi-weekly or monthly, living within the means of the other ninety percent, while yet able to give to the needs of others. Understanding that the true blessings of God are spiritual, of which is the divine favor of the Lord, and is conditional, and is given to them that obey Him. Will cause us not to seek after the things that are seen, and temporal, but the unseen, and eternal. Job said to God:

> *Thou hast granted me life and favour, and thy visitation* **[care]** *hath preserved my spirit* (Job 10:12).

Job was given favour of God, because the Bible says Job was perfect (mature), upright (blameless), one that feared God, and he avoided evil. The gift and true spiritual blessings of God are eternal life, the gifts and callings, the fruit of the Spirit, and the many great and precious promises of God. Scripture therefore says in James 1:23-27:

> *For if any be a hearer of the word, and not a doer, he is like unto a man beholding his natural face in a glass: For he beholdeth himself, and goeth his way, and straightway forgetteth what manner of man he was. But whoso looketh into the perfect law of liberty,*

62

*and continueth therein, he being not a for-getful hearer, but a doer of the work, this man **shall be blessed in his deed.***

The apostle James also give us a description of true religion. He says:

*If any man among you seem to be religious, and bridleth not his tongue, but deceiveth his own heart, this man's religion is vain. Pure religion and undefiled before God and the Father is this, To visit the fatherless and widows in their affliction, and **to keep himself unspotted from the world*** (James 1:26-27).

We are to surrender our will to God in order for us to obey Him. Without the surrender of our will to God. We will remain self-conscious, and not God conscious. We must come to understand the function of our minds. Understanding that the mind houses the intellect, emotions, and will. Without knowledge of God's word we will remain conforming to this world, its systems, moral values, attitudes, and dispositions. The word of God is what transforms, and renews our mind. As we receive knowledge of God's word and implement it in our lives, we take on the servitude of Christ, who scripture says in, Philippians 2:6, He, speaking of Jesus: *"...thought it not robbery to be equal with God, but humbled himself as a servant, and became obedient to God, even unto the death of the cross."* Scripture says that He learned obedience by the things which He suffered. We no longer have to suffer for our sins. Christ has paid the price in full. We are to suffer for the sake of the gospel.

Also, we must become aware that we are engaged in a spiritual war. 2 Corinthians 10:3-6 says:

> *For though we walk in the flesh, we do not war after the flesh: (For the weapons of our warfare are not carnal, but mighty through God to the pulling down of strong holds;)* **[mind sets]** *Casting down imaginations, and every high thing that exalteth itself against the knowledge of God, and bringing into captivity every thought to the obedience of Christ; And having in a readiness to revenge* **[punish]** *all disobedience, when your obedience is fulfilled.*

Our walk is a spiritual walk even though we live in a fleshly body. Satan's forces attack our minds because our thoughts lead to actions, and our actions lead to behavior, and our behavior is the sum total of our character. He attacks our mind because this is where the battle is waged to hinder us from serving God. He knows that we must bring our conduct under the obedience of Christ. When we are walking in sin, we open the door to satanic influences. So only when our obedience is accomplished, we than can deal with others to correct their disobedience (Matthew 7:3-5).

The apostle Paul tells us in Ephesians 6:10-18,

> *Finally, my brethren, be strong in the Lord, and in the power of his might. Put on the whole armour of God, that ye may be able to stand against the wiles of the devil. For we wrestle not against flesh and blood, but against principalities, against powers, against the rulers of the darkness of this world, against spiritual wickedness in high places.*

This all is in reference to governmental agencies, worldly systems of things, ungodly leaders, and wicked people in high authority.

But we are not to despair, because we are to be followers of God and walk in love, as Christ loves us. Separating ourselves from the sin of fornication, all uncleanliness, covetousness, filthiness, and foolish talking and jesting (joking) which are not convenient (fitting), but rather we are to give thanks to God.   For such as those who do these things, no whoremonger, nor unclean person, or idolater have no inheritance in the kingdom of Christ and of God. We are not to let anyone deceive us with vain words, because of these things the wrath of God will come on the children of disobedience. So we are not to practice sin, but walk in holiness, perfecting godliness. Knowing that we were in darkness, but now we are the children of light, we are to walk as children of light (Ephesians 5:1-10; Romans 12:1-2).

> *For the fruit of the Spirit is in all goodness*
> *and righteousness and truth; Proving what*
> *is acceptable unto the Lord* (Ephesians 5:9).

In our obedience to God, we are commanded to honor His sovereign authority and power as our Creator. Malachi 3:8 says:

> *Will a man rob God? Yet ye have robbed me.*
> *But ye say wherein have we robbed thee? In*
> *tithes and offering.*

The tithe belongs to God. We learn to give by trusting God. Therefore, Jesus instructs us in Mark 12:17, by saying:

> *Render to Caesar the things* **[our taxes]**
> *that are Caesar's, and to God the things* [the tithe, worship, praise, honor, and glory] *that are God's.*

We also learn to be content, through gratitude. Paul says in Philippians 4:11,

> *Not that I speak in respect of want: for I have*
> *learned, in whatsoever state I am, therewith*
> *to be content.*

Paul knew that his life was in Christ, so when it came to his needs being met, he knew that God would supply every need. He was so confident in God that he told the church, in verse 19,

> *But my God shall supply all your needs ac-*
> *cording to his riches in glory by Christ Je-*
> *sus.*

Our focus should not entirely be on the accumulating of material possessions, but on the things of God. We need God's wisdom, knowledge, and understanding. Jesus him-self says:

> *Take heed, and beware of covetousness: for*
> *a man's life consisteth not in the abundance*
> *of the things which he possesseth.*

Our life is in Christ!

Therefore, we are to manage our incomes God's way. We can be on public assistance, and be successful in the eyes of God. It's not the amount of money we have that deter-mines our success, but how we use it to glorify God. From a Biblical perspective, having money and material posses-sions does not make us financially successful. Believers and unbelievers alike both have fine homes, which are finished from room to room, brand new cars, and stylist clothing, to go along with silver, gold, and diamonds. We can have our heart's desire. But, if our life is not rich in the spiritual things of God, and our souls are not save, we have nothing. In the parable of the certain rich man who, because of his abundance, pulled down his barns and built greater ones to bestow all of his fruits, and goods, God required his soul, for he was not rich toward God (Luke 12:13-21).

> *For what shall it profit a man, to gain the whole world, and lose his own soul?* (Mark 8:36)

> *For all these things do the nations of the world seek after: and your Father knoweth that ye have need of these things* (Luke 12:30).

God makes the difference between our success and failure.

In order for us to be successful in our finances or even in our businesses, we must believe, trust, and obey God completely. We must keep in mind that we serve a Supernatural God, and obedience places in motion the word to be accomplished in our lives. So the first step toward becoming financially successful in the eyes of God will take faith and determination. The second step will take discipline and self-control. The third step requires having a giving heart, because God measures our giving. Scripture says in Luke 6:38:

> *Give and it shall be given unto you; good measure, pressed down, and shaken together, and running over, shall men give into your bosom. For with the same measure that ye mete withal it shall be measured to you again.*

I believe the yardstick that measures our growth, is our giving. It says to God that we trust, and depend on Him. I truly believe that God is not only speaking of our monetary giving, but also the giving of our gifts, talents, and time.

Section II - Becoming Financially Successfully

The world on the other hand, believes that financial suc cess is the accumulation of monetary and material possessions. It divides people into three classes: the poor, middle class, and the wealthy. But, for the people of God, a person earning an income of ten thousand dollars a year is finan cially successful if he or she is able to implement the three steps I have mentioned above, and likewise others who earn more or less income. [Is] Wisdom is the principle thing; therefore get wisdom: and with all thy getting get understanding [is] (Proverbs 4:7).

The world's perspective for many people mirrors failure. Jesus again warns us of covetousness when He said in Luke 12:15,

> *Take heed, and beware of covetousness: for*
> *a man's life consisteth not in the abundance*
> *of the things which he possesseth.*

We must understand that our life is in Christ. That's why the poor accumulate stuff. Their homes are piled with unnecessary stuff. In every nook and cranny you see stuff. They are made to feel that something is better then nothing. Whereas, the middle class accumulates liabilities; all their hard earn money goes to paying off debt. They have the nice homes, cars, expensive clothing. But some—not all— are knee high in debt, which is bondage. Then we have the wealthy class, which accumulates assets. An asset is anything you can convert to cash easily, something of material value. But they too have financial problems because they trust in their wealth, and not God.

When the blessing (divine favor) of the LORD is upon our lives, He makes us rich, and He adds no sorrow with it (Proverbs 10:22). Remember, joy is a fruit of the Spirit, and the fruit of the Spirit is produced in all goodness, righteousness, and truth, showing forth our walk of obedience. In our own efforts, we sometimes struggle to make ends meet,

because we have not discipline ourselves, and we have not
developed self-control. But, when the Lord blesses us by
adding to us. We will have no problem paying our mort-
gages, or car notes. We will not have a problem in the keeping of our expenditures, simply because God not only bless
us, He teaches us how to manage our Income wisely, as we
trust, and seek Him for wisdom. In other words, we recognize and honor the Lord as our source. Paul admonishes us
in saying:

> But my God shall supply all of your need ac-
> cording to his riches in glory by Christ Jesus
> (Philippians 4:19).

and 1 Corinthians 10:26 says:

> **For the earth is the Lord's, and the
> fullness thereof.**

Everything that we have belongs to the Lord! Contentment is a learned behavior, and a thankful heart of gratitude
is what enables the soul to be content. Hebrews 13:5 says:

> Let your conversation (conduct) be with-
> out covetousness; and be content with such
> things as ye have: for he hath said, **I will
> never leave thee, nor forsake thee.**

Paul told Timothy:

> For we brought nothing into this world, and
> it is certain we can carry nothing out. And
> having food and raiment let us be therewith
> content. But they that will be rich fall into
> temptation and a snare, and into many fool-
> ish and hurtful lusts, which drown men in de-
> struction and perdition (1 Timothy 6:7-9).

69

King Solomon in Ecclesiastes 10:19 makes known that: *"A feast is made for laughter, and wine maketh merry: but money answerth all things."* Money is the source we use to secure our needs, and is not to be worshipped, neither should it control us. Paul is saying to Timothy, that the very desire to be rich will cause us to fall, and become snared. Living foolishly, and allowing our hurtful or harmful lusts to dictate our lives, will cause one to err from the faith, as we see in the next verses.

Paul goes on the tell Timothy why so many live foolishly. He says:

> *For the love of money is the root of all evil: which while some coveted after, they have erred from the faith, and pierced themselves through with many sorrows* (1 Timothy 6:10).

Now Paul gives Timothy the solution to avoid being en-snared by the power of money. He says:

> *But thou, O man of God, flee these things; and follow after righteousness, godliness, faith, love, patience, meekness. Fight the good fight of faith, lay hold on eternal life, whereunto thou art also called, and hast professed a good profession before many witnesses* (1 Timothy 6:11-12).

Financial success from a biblical perspective is learning to obey God in the things concerning us financially, accord ing to the truth of God's word. We all have accomplished things in our natural lives, which have made us feel success-ful. There is no difference when it comes to our spiritual lives, and the things of God. When we walk in obedience we are walking in power, and have the victory, because we choose to serve the Victor, Christ Jesus. When we are walking in disobedience, we are living defeated lives and are walking according to the prince of the power of the air, the spirit that now works in the children of disobedience.

Jesus has made us alive in Him, and we are no longer dead in our trespasses and sin (Ephesians 2:1-7).

The world is walking in darkness, and cannot see how the devil is destroying their lives. Many who even profess Christ, allow the devil to deceive them through the sin, they allow in their lives. 2 Corinthians 4:3-10 says:

> But if our gospel be hid, it is hid to them that are lost: In whom the god of this world hath blinded the minds of them which believe not, lest the light of the glorious gospel of Christ, who is the image of God, should shine unto them. For we preach not ourselves, but Christ Jesus the Lord; and ourselves your servants for Jesus' sake. For God, who commanded the light to shine out of darkness, hath shined in our hearts, to give the light of the knowledge of the glory of God in the face of Jesus Christ. But we have this treasure in earthen vessels, that the excellency of the power may be of God, and not of us. We are troubled on every side, yet not distressed; we are perplexed, but not in despair; Persecuted, but not forsaken; cast down, but not destroyed; Always bearing about in the body the dying of the Lord Jesus, that the life also of Jesus might be made manifest in our body.

We have power over sin in our lives through the Holy Ghost who resides in us, and we no longer have to walk according to the course of this world. We have been made free from the curse of sin and death. Jesus obtained the victory over death, hell, and the grave, and without this knowledge, we would have remained in our sins, as with those who are still lost. God has saved those who have heard the gospel and believed, by grace through faith. Ephesians 2:8-10 says:

> *For by grace are ye saved through faith; and that not of yourselves: it is the gift of God: Not of works, lest any man should boast. For we are his workmanship, created in Christ Jesus unto good works, which God hath before ordained that we should walk in them.*

Rather than pursuing after God, the world is pursuing after the things that are seen. The world are pursuing after the things that are temporal. The apostle Paul tells us:

> *While we look not at the things which are seen, but at the things which are not seen: for the things which are seen are temporal; but the things which are not seen are eternal* (2 Corinthians 4:18).

> *For our light affliction, which is but for a moment, worketh for us a far more exceeding and eternal weight of glory;* (2 Corinthians 4:17).

> *For this cause we faint not; but though our outward man perish, yet the inward man is renewed day by day* (2 Corinthians 4:16).

> *Knowing that he which raised up the Lord Jesus shall raise up us also by Jesus, and shall present us with you* (2 Corinthians 4:14).

*We having the same spirit of faith, according as it is written, **I believed, and therefore have I spoken;** we also believe, and therefore speak* (2 Corinthians 4:13).

For all things are for your sakes, that the abundant grace might through thanksgiving of many redound to the glory of God (2 Corinthians 4:15).

God's word is awesome. We have so many other things we should be pursuing after as the apostle Paul clearly tell us. But so many of God's children are pursuing the blessings, and not God who blesses us. Many are rich materially, but not spiritually. If only our goal was to pursue God, it would be the ultimate of success.

✝

—6—

Becoming Financially Successful

This book of the law shall not depart out of thy mouth; but thou shalt meditate therein day and night, that thou mayest observe to do according to all that is written therein: for then thou shalt make thy way prosperous, and then thou shalt have good success (Joshua 1:8).

Becoming financially successful from a Biblical perspective is intentional obedience. We have been given three spiritual tools, or exercises, to help us grow to maturity, so that we may learn to manage our income God's way. Managing our income God's way is what makes the believer financially successful. There are three steps to becoming financially successful in the eyes of God. These steps are progressive, which means actions that are on-going, and they grow us to maturity. The first step is trusting God. The first step is difficult for many because they do not really trust God, but are solely dependent on self, attributing their success to their own efforts and not to God. The second step is living within one's means. The second step is even more difficult if you are not giving God the tithe, which honors the sovereign authority and power of God. Thereby, releasing God's divine favor in our lives, and now we are to learn to live within the other ninety percent, while yet giving to the needs of others, which is the third step. We are to ask and seek God for wisdom, knowledge, and understanding, so that we can live a life of self-control, and discipline through our praying and fasting.

Becoming financially successful from a Biblical perspec tive is putting forth a conscious effort to obey God. In do- ing so, God will prosper us because of our obedience. The same effort and ambitions we put forth to accomplish suc- cess by the world's standard is the same that we should put forth when it comes to the things of God. Oftentimes we fail to obey, because we become hearers of the word, and not doers, only to deceive ourselves in believing that we are truly trusting God, not really understanding what it means to trust Him.

As we know, the book that is spoken of in this text is the book of the law, which contained the oracles of God. Josh- ua, during that time, was instructed of the LORD to medi- tate day and night that which was written in the law, to un- derstand that he must first know what is in the law, thereby enabling him to observe the law. So Joshua, you need to know what you are to observe, and the result of you observ- ing what is written in the book of the law will make your way prosperous, and then you will have good success.

Similar to this text, The Apostle Paul tells us to:

> *Study to show thyself approved unto God, a workman that needeth not to be ashamed, rightly dividing the word of truth* (2 Timothy 2:15).

The study that Paul is speaking of demands the total ef- fort of our mind, emotions, and will. God's word must prop- erly be interpreted by rightly dividing it. Study involves praying that God may enlighten the understanding. It in- volves entering into the presence of God, so that the Holy Spirit can help us understand the truth of God's Word. Paul says:

For they that are after the flesh do mind the things of the flesh; but they that are after the Spirit **[speaking of the obedient child of God]** *the things of the Spirit. For to be carnally minded [is] death; but to be spiritually minded [is] life and peace. Because the carnal mind [is] enmity against God: for it is not subject to the law of God, neither indeed can be.* **[Speaking of the law of the Spirit of life which make us free to walk in the Spirit, which mean being led of God's Spirit]** *So then they that are in the flesh cannot please God. But ye are not in the flesh,•***[speaking of the obedient child of God]** *but in the Spirit, if so be that the Spirit of God dwell in you. Now if any man have not the Spirit of Christ, he is none of his. And if Christ [be] in you, the body [is] dead because of sin; but the Spirit [is] life because of righteousness* (Romans 8:5-10).

With all that said, the born-again believer now has a new nature, and must grow to maturity by implementing the word of God in his or her life. The old sin nature died with Christ on the cross, which Paul tells us about in Romans 6:4-13, but sin he said reigns in our mortal bodies, and for us to crucify the flesh, and to walk in the new nature which is created after the righteousness of God (Ephesians 4:24). Jesus teaches us to watch and pray unless we enter into temptation. For the spirit truly is ready (or willing), but the flesh (lusts of) is weak (Mark 14:38). If we walk after the flesh, are walking in sin or darkness. If we are walking after the Spirit we walk in the light or the newness of life. Which one we yield to is the one that will dictate and dominate our life. The new nature and the flesh struggles, or wars with or against one another. Choosing to walk in the Spirit (being led by God's Spirit) is making the choice of living in obedience to God. We must be born of God's Spirit to live a holy life, and the reason so many are not living a holy life even though they have been born-again are yet walking in the flesh, and not the Spirit, which makes it impossible for them to live holy. Read also Ephesians 4:20-30.

Our physical bodies are nurtured by the physical food we eat. Eating the right food helps us to grow and develop into healthy and strong individuals. Likewise, our new nature needs to be fed the word of God that we may grow into healthy and strong, mature Christians. So Paul again says:

> *Wherefore laying aside all malice* **[ill-will]**, *and all guile* **[cunningness]**, *and all hypocrisies* **[false pretense]** *and envies* **[discontent excited by superiority of another's prosperity]**, *and all evil speaking. As newborn babes, desire the sincere milk of the word that ye may grow thereby: If so be ye have tasted that the Lord is gracious* (1 Peter 2:1-3).

Desire initiates our growth in the spirit, and lust hinders it. The desire to live a holy and righteous life will cause the born-again believer to seek God's word. We know that the Lord is good. But are we willing to give up what we think is good, for what the Lord has reserved for those who love Him, and keep his commands? Jesus says:

> *If ye love me, keep my commandments. And I will pray the Father, and he shall give you another Comforter, that he may abide with you for ever; Even the Spirit of truth; whom the world cannot receive, because it seeth him not, neither knoweth him: but ye know*

*him; for he dwelleth with you, and shall be
in you* (John 14:15-17).

The Spirit of God, which is Love, residing in the believer not only enables us to love God, but also one another, and even our enemies. Therefore, our love for God is what causes us to obey. If we have not learned obedience, it is because of something or someone we value more.

A lawyer who was tempting Jesus, asked a question about the great commandment:

> *Master, which [is] the great commandment in the law? Jesus said unto him,* **Thou shalt love the Lord thy God with all thy heart, and with all thy soul, and with all thy mind.** *This is the first and great commandment. And the second [is] like unto it,* **Thou shalt love thy neighbour as thyself.** *On these two commandments hang all the law and the prophets.* (Matthew 22:36-40).

Keeping these two commandments is the fulfilling of the Law, which are no longer on tables of stone, but have been written in our heart, as the result of the new birth, and under the new covenant. We are a part of the new covenant, because we are the seed of Abraham, by faith. Jesus Christ is the lineage that connects us to Abraham. We have been born of God's seed, and are not to habitually practice sin (Matthew 22:36-40; Hebrews 8:7-10;,Romans 4:13-22). 1 John 3:9 says:

> *Whosoever is born of God doth not commit sin; for his seed remaineth in him: and he cannot sin, because he is born of God.*

It is now possible for us to not be controlled by our emotions or the flesh. But, we can walk in the fruit of the Spirit. Galatians 5:22-25 says:

> *But the fruit of the Spirit is love, joy, peace, longsuffering, gentleness, goodness, faith, Meekness, temperance: against such there is no law. And they that are Christ's have crucified the flesh with the affections and lusts. If we live in the Spirit, let us also walk in the Spirit.*

God grew me through my trust in Him. Your need may be in another areas, it was my finances. I came from a fam ily of sixteen children, of whom I am now the oldest, two are deceased. My desire to be rich was so strong that I was driven by blind ambition. I did pursue my career to no avail. I wanted a career in Finances as an accountant, a consultant, or as a financial counselor. It's a long story. God would not allow my success in these areas, and as I began seeking God, and in trusting and pursuing Him, my purpose was revealed to me. He has called me to teach, and preach the gospel of the kingdom of God. In my progression of spiritual growth, God abducted me into the military, for the purpose of teaching me spiritual warfare. I served 11 years in the Army National Guard before I became ill, from my tour in the Gulf War, in which I also have experienced God's power as my Healer.

The first step toward becoming financially successful will take faith and determination. Each of us has been given a measure of faith. Faith is not only a gift, it is also one of the Fruit of the Spirit. We must put our faith in God, and not in other things. When we seek God in faith, the Bible says He is pleased with us. Listen, Hebrews 11:1 says:

Now faith is the substance of things hoped for, the evidence of things not seen.

But, without faith it is impossible to please him; for he that cometh to God must believe that he is, and that he is a rewarder of them that diligently seek him (Hebrews 11:6).

Notice carefully, that Jesus tells us in the sixth chapter of Matthew, that if we give, pray, and fast in secret, the Father who see in secret will openly reward us. God is a rewarder of them that diligently seek him. Reward means, something offered for service or achievement. God offers us righteousness, peace, and joy in the Holy Ghost, through our acceptance of Jesus Christ (Romans 8:32, 2 Corinthians 5:21, Isaiah 26:3; Psalms 16:11). If we are going to become financially successfully God's way, we must have faith, and we must learn to trust God. We do that by getting to know Him, spending time with Him in prayer. Prayer is a spiritual tool or exercise that we use to connect with God, in our relationship with Him. Prayer is talking, and listening to God, and God listening and talking to us.

In prayer we ask, seek, and knock. Jesus tells us to:

Ask, and it shall be given you; seek, and ye shall find; knock, and it shall be opened unto you: For every one that asketh receiveth; and he that seeketh findeth; and to him that knocketh it shall be open. Or what man is there of you, whom if his son ask bread, will he give him a stone? Or if he ask a fish, will he give him a serpent? If ye then, being evil, know how to give good gifts unto your children, how much more shall your Father which is in heaven give good things to them that ask him? (Matthew 7:7-11)

80

So then, when we pray, we must believe that God is who He says He is, and that He will reward us for diligently seeking Him. The word diligent means showing painstaking effort and application in whatever is undertaken. The word of God is to be sought after, and then applied to our lives. Therefore, the Bible says to have faith in God, to act upon His word. Now when we come to Him not really believing He is able to do what we have asked of Him, this is not faith, but doubt. We should pray believing what we have asked of Him, according to His will, that we will receive it, because God has already done what we have asked of Him. We must now wait on its manifestation.

Scripture says in 1 John 5:14-15 that:

> *This is the confidence that we have in him, that, if we ask any thing according to his will, he heareth us: And if we know that he hear us, whatsoever we ask, we know that we have the petitions that we desired of him.*

I am not rich or wealthy according to the standard of the world. But I am rich according to Proverbs 10:22, I am rich in the LORD, and He has not added any sorrow with it. When I first began to really trust God, He told me "not to go by what I see, feel, or think." I must stand on His word. I had to rise above my situations, and circumstances. I had to trust God in whatever state I was in, not going by what I saw, thought or felt. I had to stand on the Word of God. Isaiah 40:6-7 says:

> *The grass withereth, the flower fadeth: be cause the spirit of the LORD bloweth upon it: surely the people is grass. The grass withereth, the flower fadeth: but the word of our God shall stand for ever.*

It was not enough for me to believe God. I had to learn how to be patient, or wait on the Lord. So no matter what things appeared to be surrounding my circumstance or situations, I knew God would answer my prayers, because my confidence was in Him.

What exactly is patience? Patience is the ability to accept delays and to endure waiting without complaining. Spiritual growth is a process, and requires us to learn patience. Our expectation is of the Lord; therefore we must learn to wait patiently on the guidance, and the instructions God gives us through the written word, and by way of the Holy Spirit. The psalmist says:

> *Truly my soul waiteth upon God: from him cometh my salvation* (Psalm 62:1).

> *My soul, wait thou only upon God; for my expectation is from him. He only is my rock and my salvation: he is my defense; I shall not be moved. In God is my salvation and my glory: the rock of my strength, and my refuge, is in God. Trust in him at all times; ye people, pour out your heart before him: God is a refuge for us. Selah* (Psalm 5-8).

We must learn to wait patiently on the Lord, and not be moved by what we see, feel or think. Romans 8:24-28 says:

> *For we are saved by hope: but hope that is seen is not hope: for what a man seeth, why doth he yet hope for? But if we hope for that we see not, then do we with patience wait for it. Likewise the Spirit also helpeth our infirmities: for we know not what we should pray for as we ought: but the Spirit itself*

maketh intercession for us with groanings which cannot be uttered. And he that searcheth the hearts knoweth what is the mind of the Spirit, because he maketh intercession for the saints according to the will of God. And we know that all things work together for good to them that love God, to them who are the called according to his purpose. For whom he did foreknow, he also did predestinate, to be conformed to the image of his Son, that he might be the firstborn among many brethren.

We must believe what God's word says, and not doubt in our hearts. The word of God is a sure foundation, and our hope is in Jesus Christ, the rock of our salvation. Our determination should be to please Him, and this is only done by walking in faith, while obeying and trusting God's guidance in our lives.

Fasting on the other hand, is communing with God. Fasting is voluntarily refraining from food and/or drink for a time to give us opportunity to give our full attention to God, concerning a particular matter. It must be accompanied with sincere prayer, to be effective in securing an answer from God. It is the denial of self, which humbles the soul. It is a spiritual exercise that God has designed for each of us, which disciplines the body. David says in Psalm 35:12-13,

They rewarded me evil for good to the spoiling of my soul. But as for me, when they were sick, my clothing was sackcloth: I humbled my soul with fasting; and my prayer returned into mine own bosom.

Section II - Becoming Financially Successfully

David said, even though I was treated evil, for my good, when I would pray for those who were sick, the prayer in my heart would be for myself. Fasting is a cleansing process which, from the beginning to the end, cleanses our spirit, mind, and body all at the same time. Fasting also is a divine corrective to the pride of the human heart. It is instrumental in our obedience to God.

It is a discipline of the body, with the tendency to humble the soul. We develop self-control through denial. Fasting can alter our lives in such a way that we are able to move in new freedom, new closeness to God, and new unity with our fellowmen. Obeying the Lord, and seeking a closer walk with Him through the regular discipline of prayer and fasting is worth the reward God has promised us (Isaiah 58:6-11). Fasting brings us into a greater knowledge of God, and releases us into the fullness, and power of the Holy Spirit's work in our lives, and it brings us to the point of greater health.

What do the Scriptures say about fasting?

> *Moreover when you fast, be not, as the hypocrites, of a sad countenance: for they disfigure their faces, that they may appear unto men to fast. Verily I say unto you, They have their reward. But thou, when thou fastest, anoint thine head, and wash thy face; That thou appear not unto men to fast, but unto thy Father which is in secret: and thy Father, which seeth in secret, shall reward thee openly* (Matthew 6:16-18).

No one should know you are fasting, except your husband or wife, for the scripture says:

> *The wife hath not power of her own body, but the husband: and likewise also the hus-*

> *band hath not power of his own body, but the*
> *wife. Defraud ye not one the other, except it*
> *be with consent for a time, that ye may give*
> *yourselves to fasting and prayer; and come*
> *together again, that Satan tempt you not for*
> *your incontinency* (1 Corinthians 7:4-5).

Other people can be told politely, when asked the reason for not eating, "I have turned my plate down." The benefits of fasting are that it humbles the soul and disciplines our bodies. It purges our spirit, and gives force to our prayers. Fasting releases our faith for healing, and it brings deliverance.

How then do we fast? Gradually. Designate a day and begin with a six hour fast, from noon to 6pm, until you are able to do a twelve hour fast, from 6am to 6pm. Then continue until you are able to do a twenty-four hour fast from your designated day at 6pm to 6pm the next day. For those of you who take medication, your fast time will revolve around your intake of medication. For example, if you choose to fast from 12 o'clock noon to 6 o'clock in the evening, and your medication is scheduled at 3 o'clock pm, you would eat at that time, enough to take your medication. For example, you would have some soup, or pasta, a dish of wholesome vegetables, or a baked potato. This is done each time your medication is scheduled during your designated fast day.

During your designated fast, drink distilled or spring water only, if possible. It is better then faucet water, because it draws the toxins out of your cells. Always begin and end your fast with prayer. Whenever possible, use this time to read and study the word of God, having a specific purpose for fasting. For example, for spiritual understanding, for healing, for deliverance, for guidance and directions, for a loved one to be saved, for financial blessing, wisdom, spiritual growth, or for the main purpose of receiving answer to prayer. If you should end before your designated time, do not feel defeated. Continue fasting each week, until you have disciplined yourself, to fast one complete day. After then, fast each week on your designated day. For example, if you would like your fast day to be on Wednesday of each week, your fast would begin on Tuesday at 6pm, and it would end Wednesday at 6pm. Check with your doctor before you begin to fast.

Time with God is your objective. Remain in a spirit of prayer throughout the day, making melody in your heart to the Lord, giving thanks always. You are ministering to the Lord. You are giving your full attention to God. You are allowing the Spirit to dominate the body. The benefits of fasting again are: it cleanses your spirit, mind, and body, and it humbles the soul.

✝

SCRIPTURE REFERENCES TO FASTING

When to fast	Mark 2:18-20 (now)
How to fast	Matthew 6:16-18 1 Corinthians 7:4-5
Fasting humbles the soul	Psalm 35:13
Fasting afflicts the soul	Isaiah 58:5
Gives force to our prayer	2 Chronicles 7:14
Spiritual efficacy of fasting	Mark 9:29
The acceptable fast	Isaiah 58:3-7
Promise/reward for sincere fast	Isaiah 58:8-12
Public fasts	Joel 1:13-14 Joel 2:12 James 4:9
Private fasts Jesus	Matthew 4:1; Mark 1:12-13; Luke 4:1-2
Moses	Deuteronomy 9:9; 18
Elijah	1 Kings 19:8
Hezekiah	Isaiah 31:1-3
Daniel	Daniel 10:2-3
Esther	Esther 4:15-17

Section III

Steps to Financial Freedom

—7—
Step One - Trusting God

Trust in the Lord with all thine heart; and lean not unto thine own understanding. In all thy ways acknowledge him, and he shall direct thy paths (Proverbs 3:5-6).

Trusting God is the first step to becoming financially suc cessful from a biblical perspective. The area of finances is sometimes the most pressing difficulties facing the believer, because we have not learned how to develop self-control and discipline. Courage, on the other hand, is the ability to face difficulty or danger with firmness, and without fear. When we trust God, we receive courage to face the uncertainties of life. It is difficult to be relaxed and efficient at work when one is perpetually worried about finances. Financial prob lems come because of our attitudes toward money, and our inefficiencies in handling it wisely. We must view money realistically. In one of Jesus' parables, he described a man whose life had been spent in the accumulation of wealth. Then the man died, unprepared to meet God and forced to leave his precious possessions to someone else. Jesus called this man a fool. He was rich in worldly possessions, but poor in his relationship with God (Luke 2:16-21).

God gives us the ability to prosper, to become wealthy, or He sometimes, only supplies our needs, and expects us to trust Him. This was clearly seen in the life of the Prophet Elijah (Deuteronomy 8:17; 1 king 17; 3 John 2). In Phi lippians 4:19, the apostle Paul tells us that we need not be anxious or worried about having enough, and Jesus made known that a life of obedience brings the providence of God into our lives. Jesus says:

But seek ye first the kingdom of God and his righteousness; and all these things shall be added unto you (Matthew 6:33).

There are people who squander their hard earn money through mismanagement, and others who confuse their real needs with their desires. In terms of the basic necessities of life, God provides and often in great abundance. For reasons known only to Him, He sometimes permits hunger and financial hardship, even among His faithful followers (Philippians 4:19; Mark 6:7-11; Matthew 6:25-34).

Money and possessions can also be a hindrance to our spiritual growth. The rich young ruler who came to Jesus desiring to follow Him, walked away grieving when he heard the command to give all that he had to the poor. Apparently, a love for money prevented his spiritual growth. He was learning as Jesus said on another occasion, that one could gain the whole world and loose his soul. Jesus also taught that we couldn't love both God and money. Eventually we will come to the point of loving the one, and hating the other. A love of money can stifle spiritual growth and can prevent our turning to Christ (Matthew 19:16-24; Mark 8:36; Matthew 6:24, Deuteronomy 8:11-14).

We should manage our finances wisely. In the parable of the talents, Jesus warns us about the mismanagement of our resources and ends with the unfaithful servant being separated from his friends and master. Money management principles can be found in this parable. 1] that God entrusts resources to us in many forms, especially financially. 2] that God give these resources to his servants in different amounts. 3] that God expects us to plan and manage our resources with the goal of making a profit, and 4] that God condemns laziness or anxiety in our financial planning.

In trusting God, we must come to realize that everything that is made was made by Him, and for Him. There is nothing that was not made by Him, and that all things consist in Him. He has the power and authority to give us everything we need, and desire in our heart. Even though God is sovereign, some of His blessings are conditional (John 1:1-3; Deuteronomy 28). The key to trusting God is obedience. When God speaks to our hearts. He wants us to obey.

I experienced life's disappointments throughout my growing years, and did not understand how to trust. The reality of the fact that life is not fair had disappointed me so, that when it came to God, I had no knowledge of how to trust. I remember telling the Lord, I want to trust you, but I don't know how to trust. There are many who really do not know how to trust the Lord. They have become afraid of placing their trust in another, and its called fear. Faith in God is trusting Him.

The mind has a way of shutting down. We can be totally unaware of something that we are doing. Yet, others can see what we cannot see. The perfect example of this is a person that is addicted to drugs. The chronic drug addict is blinded by the need of drugs; he or she does not care whether they hurt anyone, or cause hardship, as long as their need is satisfied.

In my circumstances, my mind had been blinded by so much disappointment, that I only trusted my mother, grandmother, older brother, Willie and my church families. At the time, I could not identify with what I was doing. I was the second oldest of sixteen children, and missed what it was like being a child. I grew up fast, as far as having the responsibilities of caring for my younger siblings. Going to church was all I really had to look forward too, in a sense. My time spent away from home, was with my God families, and I really didn't understanding then, that I trusted them. God was teaching me how to trust. Yet, I was unaware of what I was doing.

We learn to trust others by their reputation. A person's word was considered binding. Now days, its so easy to go back on our word, for any number of reasons. We learn to trust others by recommendation. I know a person, so I recommend this person to you. You can then choose to take my word or not concerning this person. We learn to trust others simply by getting to know them. We establish a relationship, spend time getting to know the person, therefore our knowledge and experience is what determines whether we can trust or not trust them. All these are similar ways we are encouraged to know and trust God. The last way is the right way! Seeking God is the first step in trusting Him.

Trust in the Lord with all thine heart; and lean not unto thine own understanding (Proverbs 3:5).

The scripture above tells us whom to trust specifically. The Psalmist says to trust in the Lord, indicating that there are many other things which we can erroneously put our trust. We can even depend solely on ourselves. We not only are told whom to trust, but how we are to trust, with all our heart. Our heart is our innermost being. It is the seat of our emotions. He tells us to trust the Lord with our entire heart. We are also told in this verse, to lean not to our own understanding, but in all our ways we are to acknowledge the Lord. We acknowledge the Lord through our giving, prayer, and fasting. We acknowledge that He is Lord over our lives. We acknowledge that everything that is made, was made by Him, and for Him. We do not belong to ourselves, we have been brought with a price. Not with silver, nor gold, but with the precious blood of the Lamb, Jesus Christ Himself, our Savior.

In our walk with the Lord, there will be things happening to us that we may not understand. It is in our not understanding, that we are to seek the Lord. This is why it is so important for us to read the word of God every day. It enables us to become familiar with what is in God's word, then the Holy Spirit will bring to our remembrance, what we need and when we need it.

93

I had no knowledge of spiritual warfare; therefore I did not know that the unseen forces that came against me purpose was to kill, steal, and to destroy me. But, my faith in the Lord would always cause me to pray, and seek His face, even in my backslidden condition.

When our **will** has been taken into captivity by the trickery of the devil, God wants us to turn away from sin, and back to Him, so that we can do His **will** and not the **will** of the devil. Often He accomplishes this by using His servants to gently redirect the actions of those caught up in the snares of the devil, by instruction as stated in 2 Timothy 2:24-26:

> *And the servant of the Lord must not strive; but be gentle unto all men, apt to teach, patient, In meekness instructing those that oppose themselves; if God peradventure* **[perhaps]** *will give them repentance to the acknowledging of the truth; And that they may recover themselves out of the snare of the devil, who are taken captive by him at (to do) his will.*

Even though our **will** may be bound up, our emotions still can be expressed. This is why we can say we love Jesus, and disobey His word. God, through prayer and deliverance will set our **will** free, so that we can make Jesus Christ our choice, and when God deliver us, the results is repentance. So then, we must not only trust the Lord. But we must also seek to understand the word of God concerning our lives.

In a moment I will tell you why we can trust the Lord. But right now, it is very important for us to seek the Lord, regardless of our current disobedience. What exactly do I mean? Even in our sinfulness, we are to seek the Lord. It is the acknowledging of the Lord's power that brings deliverance. In our sinfulness, we must confess our sin, ask for forgiveness, and then repent. Repentance is turning from sin, toward God. In the acknowledgement of the Lord, we say in fact that He is the only one that can help us, and that He has the power to deliver us. Once we repent, conversion should come next. Conversion is a change of mind, which results in a change of conduct. If we continue in our sin, we have not truly repented.

How many times have we tried to stop what we were doing and could not? It is difficult to understand why the Lord sometimes take so long to bring our much needed deliverance. We know our love for the Lord is real, and we do want to serve, and obey Him. We may say to the Lord, "why so Lord, do You allow me to remain in this bondage so long? Lord you have the power to set me free." It is because our **will** has been taken captive by the devil. Therefore, when the Lord does releases us from bondage, its result is twofold. First, we come to know that we are not the one responsible for the release, but God and the glory is rightly placed. Secondly, the Lord has made sure we will not return to our captivity, or bondage!

We must understand also when we are seeking the Lord we must draw closer to Him, and He will draw closer to us. James 4:6-8 says:

> *But he giveth more grace. Wherefore he saith,* *GOD **RESISTETH THE PROUD, BUT GIVETH GRACE UNTO THE HUMBLE**. Submit yourselves therefore to God. Resist the devil, and he will flee from you. Draw nigh to God, and he will draw nigh to you. Cleanse your hands, ye sinners; and purify your hearts, ye double minded.*

The doubled minded are the saved folks who have one leg in the world, and one leg in the Kingdom, who are straddling the fence. We must purify our hearts. We must get our hearts right with God. We must choose whom we are

95

going to serve. Jesus did not die for us to remain in sin. In Colossians 1:13 we are told that God has delivered us from the power of darkness, and has translated us into the kingdom of His dear son, Jesus Christ. No matter what we are seeking deliverance from, an abusive relationship, alcohol, drugs, homelessness, fornication, etcetera; God has already delivered us from it, if only we would surrender our *will* totally to Him. Remember, that when we sincerely seek the Lord, in the process of us seeking Him, He will give us guidance and direction. God's question to you, will you obey them?

What makes an obedient child obey? Realizing the value of doing what is right makes the obedient child obey. Trust and obedience then goes hand in hand. Trust is having confidence or faith in a person or thing. Trust is believing, and expecting; entrusting or depending on another. Trust is belief in action. Trusting God is surrendering our *will*, to His *will*. Our knowledge of God determines whether we will trust Him, or not. For example, a child knows a parent's love, by the care that is shown to him or her. Likewise, God demonstrated His love for us, by allowing Jesus to die on the cross for our sins. The Bible simply says: *For he hath made him [to be] sin for us, who knew no sin; that we might be made the righteousness of God in him"* (2 Corinthians 5:21). *"For when we were yet without strength, in due time Christ died for the ungodly"* (Romans 5:6).

How then do we seek the Lord? We seek the Lord in our giving, prayer, and fasting. These three spiritual tools or exercises are for the purpose of disciplining us, which develops in us devotion, communion, fellowship, and trust in God.

You may be asking about now, what does all this have to do with my financial success? I did mention earlier that the first step of financial success required faith, and determination. Our determination should be to please God. Hebrews 11:6, says:

But without faith it is impossible to please him: **for he that cometh to God must believe that he is, and that he is a rewarder of them that diligently seek him.**

There are three things we must take in account. One, our faith is what we believe. Two, God is, who God says He is. And three, God rewards those who diligently seek Him. This leads us back to Matthew 6:33, which says:

But seek ye first the kingdom of God, and his righteousness; and all these things shall be added unto you.

Jesus is speaking of our physical needs being added to us, as we seek to understand God's kingdom and as we seek to understand the righteousness of God. Sadly, instead of seeking the kingdom of God and His righteousness most of our efforts go toward accumulating material possessions, rather then spending time with the Lord. We are to pursue God, not wealth or riches.

Knowledge of someone is what helps us determine whether we can trust them. Our knowledge of God tells us that we can trust Him. Why? God is omnipotent, which means that He is almighty, and all-powerful. No one or nothing is more powerful than our God. He rules and reigns over the nations of this earth. Daniel attests to the power and authority of God:

Daniel answered and said, "Blessed be the name of God for ever and ever: for wisdom and might is his: And he changeth the times and the seasons: he removeth kings, and setteth up kings: he giveth wisdom unto the wise, and knowledge to them that know

*understanding: He revealeth the deep and
secret things: he knoweth what is in the
darkness, and the light dwelleth with him
(Daniel 2:20-22).*

God has the power and the authority to do as He pleases.
One example is Nelson Mandela's fight against apartheid.
He stood for what was right, and in his humility, God exalted him and made him president of South Africa in 1994. We
saw God's hand upon many of our leaders in history, both
white and black, which include Martin Luther King Jr., and
now Barack Obama, the first African American president of
the United States. We must understand that God has ordained government (Romans 13:1-4). God's righteousness,
even in wickedness, prevails. He uses the wicked for His
purpose and the forces of the universe are at His beck and
call (Luke 8:24). Proverbs 16:4 says:

*The LORD hath made all things for himself:
yea, even the wicked for the day of evil.*

God is Omniscient, which means He is all knowing. Can
you imagine knowing the thoughts of every individual on
this earth? Awesome! Our God is awesome. Nothing is hidden from Him. He knows every disappointment, hurt, and
pain we feel. All of the knowledge we have acquired came
from God. Our ability to create was given to us by God. He
gives men dreams and visions, and brings them to pass. All
that we see in the earth today, God allows man to create.
Jesus says in Revelation 1:8,

*I am Alpha and Omega, the beginning and
the ending, saith the Lord, which is, and
which was, and which is to come, the Almighty.*

Jesus knows everything about us.

We were known even before we were conceived. God has a plan for our lives. Who else are we to seek, but the one who has created us? Jesus tells us to follow Him for this reason. He is the way to eternal life. He says:

> *No man can come to me, except the Father which hath sent me draw him: and I will raise him up at the last day. It is written in the prophets, **and they shall be all taught of God. Every man therefore that hath heard, and hath learned of the Father, cometh unto me.** Not that any man hath seen the Father, save he which is of God, he hath seen the Father. Verily, verily, I say unto you, He that believeth on me hath everlasting life* (John 6:44-47).

We can trust Jesus, because He knows the way to God. Jesus said:

> *...I am the way, the truth and the life: no man cometh unto the Father, but by me* (John 14:6).

As we follow Jesus, we learn to overcome self, sin, and satan. In order to follow Christ, we must first deny our selves. The word deny means; "refuse to grant, refuse to give ourselves over to our lustful appetites." Jesus goes on to say in Matthew 16:24-26,

> *...If any man will come after me, let him deny himself, and take up his cross, and follow me. For whosoever will save his life shall lose it: and whosoever will lose his life for my sake shall find it. For what is a man*

*profited, if he shall gain the whole world,
and lose his own soul? or what shall a man
give in exchange for his soul?*

Therefore, pursuing after material possession is not
what God is calling us to do. God wants us to seek after His
wisdom, knowledge, and understanding; He wants us to be
rich toward Him spiritually.

God is Omnipresent, which mean He is present everywhere all the time. David said:

*Whither shall I go from thy spirit? or whith-
er shall I flee from they presence? If I ascend
up into heaven, thou art there: if I make my
bed in hell, behold, thou are there. If I take
the wings of the morning, and dwell in the
uttermost parts of the sea; Even there shall
thy hand lead me, and thy right hand shall
hold me* (Psalm 139:7-10).

God is always present in our lives. He promises that He
will never leave nor forsake us (Hebrews 13:5). Trust in the
Lord brings courage and stability. Therefore, the Lord has
given the church gifts, so that we may grow together in love
and mature spiritually enabling us to trust in Him.

✝

—8—
Step Two
Living Within One's Means

Labour not to be rich: cease from thine
own wisdom (Proverbs 23:4).

Living within one's means is the second step to becoming financially successful from a Biblical perspective. The second step will take discipline, and self-control. The word discipline means to train to improve strength or self-control, or to train by instruction or practice, especially to teach self-control. The word self-control means the act of denying yourself, controlling your impulses, or the control of one's behavior. To live within one's means takes great restraint, and the understanding of real needs. We must learn to prioritize our expenses. We can only do this by seeking God's wisdom concerning the true necessaries of life.

We must understand that money is the source we use to secure our needs, and that God's chief competitor is money, or mammon, which is the personification of riches or wealth. Jesus specifically uses this example of the other master sim ply because it is what so many people seek after and desire, rather than God. Money in and of itself is not evil, but the apostle Paul tells us in 1 Timothy 6:10, that the love of money is the root of all evil, and that many have erred from the faith, and have pierced themselves with many sorrows because of their greediness. We are to understand that,

The blessing of the Lord it maketh rich and
he add no sorrow with it (Proverbs 10:22).

101

Solomon tells us to *"labor not to be rich."* Why? It is vain, which means it is worthless. All our hard work to become rich, and the effort put forth to accumulate wealth, only to leave it for someone else to enjoy, is vanity. We are to enjoy life, and work as God's gift to man. Ecclesiastes 2:24-26 says:

> *There is nothing better for a man, than that*
> *he should eat and drink, and that he should*
> *make his soul enjoy good in his labor. This*
> *also I saw, that it was from the hand of God.*
> *For who can eat, or who else can hasten*
> *hereunto, more than I? For God giveth to*
> *a man that is good in his sight wisdom, and*
> *knowledge, and joy:* **but to the sinner he**
> **giveth travail, to gather and to heap**
> **up, that he may give to him that is**
> **good before God. This also is vanity**
> **and vexation of spirit.**

This is what scripture means when it says the wealth of the wicked is laid up for the righteous (Proverbs 13:22). God transfers or uses what money is accumulated from the wicked, and it is given to His people to further the work of the kingdom.

When we look at work as a gift from God we can enjoy our labor, and avoid the pain and suffering we experience in putting forth our own efforts to fulfill our own purposes. We are to seek God's plan for our lives, and allow Him to direct us in the way. Therefore, we must intentionally teach our young people not to forget the Creator in their youth, because this is the time, which we seek to find who we are. It is a time of discovery, when you and I should have sought God for our purpose and destiny.

Deuteronomy 8:11-14 says:

> *Beware that thou forget not the LORD thy*
> *God, in not keeping his commandments,*
> *and his judgments, and his statutes, which*
> *I command thee this day: Lest when thou*
> *hast eaten and art full, and hast built good-*
> *ly houses, and dwelt therein; And when thy*
> *herds and thy flocks multiply, and thy sil*
> *ver and thy gold is multiplied, and all that*
> *thou hast is multiplied; Then thine heart be*
> *lifted up, and thou forget the LORD thy God,*
> *which brought thee forth out of the land of*
> *Egypt, from the house of bondage.*

When we read a little further, Moses reminds the children of Israel that it was God who led and fed them in the wilderness.

Moses warned the children of Israel not to;

> *...say in thine heart, My power and the*
> *might of mine hand hath gotten me this*
> *wealth. But thou shalt remember the LORD*
> *thy God: for it is he that giveth thee power*
> *to get wealth, that he may establish his cov-*
> *enant which he sware unto thy father, as it*
> *is this day* (Deuteronomy 8:17).

The covenant that is spoken of is the Abrahamic Covenant, which is in effect today. God will show us even now our purpose and destiny. He told Jeremiah,

> *Before I formed thee in the belly I knew*
> *thee; and before thou camest forth out of the*
> *womb I sanctified thee, and I ordained thee*
> *a prophet unto the nations* (Jeremiah 1:5).

Who knows us better than the one who has created us?

103

God has a plan and purpose for our lives. Therefore, it is never too late to seek God for guidance and directions. He will help us discover our gifts, and talents. In doing so, we will enjoy our labor, as gifts from God!

It is through our obedience that God prospers us (Deuteronomy 28). Prosperity is the condition of prospering, and having good fortune. Therefore, to labor is a gift of God. We are to labor not to become wealthy, but to enjoy the work of our hands. Solomon goes on to say, *cease from thine own wisdom*. Stop living life according to your own ways. The wisdom of God, on the other hand, is priceless. It is more precious than silver or gold. It cannot be compared to rubies. Ecclesiastes 10:10 says:

> *If the iron be blunt, and he do not whet the*
> *edge, then must he put to more strength: but*
> *wisdom is profitable to direct.*

The New King James version reads,

> *If the ax is dull, and one does not sharpen*
> *the edge, Then he must use more strength;*
> *But wisdom brings success.*

Also remember now, that wisdom is a gift. It is a mental, physical, and spiritual skill. It is from God, therefore we do not become successful in our own strength, but through the strength which is given of God to create wealth. So, we are to pursue God, and not riches, or wealth, for our success. Wisdom is what makes us successful. Implementing the creative power God has given to us through ideas, gifts, and talents.

Also in Matthew 6:33, Jesus promises to provide for us as we seek first the kingdom of God, and His righteousness. Through discipline and self-control, we learn to spend wisely. Because, money is easy to spend, but to keep track of it is hard. It is hard, because we fail to put forth the effort of tracking our spending. Putting together a financial system, and setting aside time to record our expenditures is painstaking to some. So we rather just write out quickly a few reminders of what bills we have to pay. Set side the amount of money, we will be spending on our hair and nails. Tuck away the dollar we will put in church, and be on our way to buying groceries for the next couples of days. Then we sit and try to figure out why we do not have money for gas.

Men who are allowed to keep their paychecks, and are not issued an allowance. Normally, are the one who deposit their half of the expenditures in the joint bank account for their share of the bills, and with the rest of their hard earned money, prepares for the weekend. They wash their cars, fill the gas tank. Set aside money for the lotto, and what they will lose at the casino. Come Monday, are asking their wife for money to get a cup of coffee. Just a little humor!

If you are in debt, get out of debt. If you are out of debt, do not get in debt. When we are in debt, we are living outside of our means, and we are in bondage, with one exception. We have control of our spending, and we are paying down on our credit cards, or secure debt, and we are making progress in lowering our debt. We are right where God want us to be. Our trust or lack of trust in God has placed us where we are. Whether we have a low paying or sixfig ure job. Whether we are living on public assistance or living with our mothers.   We can become financially successful God's way.

To become financial successful, you begin by preparing a budget. You will need your pay stubs from the prior month. Add up the total gross income, multiply by ten percent, and that amount will be your tithe. Then you add up the total net pay amount, and deduct the tithe from the total of your net pay, and you will have your monthly budget amount. From your monthly budget amount, you will begin deducting the amount of your mortgage, or rent, home insurance if it is paid monthly. To arrive at your monthly budget for utilities, you will need the last six months of your utilities bills. Total each utility, then divide by six, adding an additional amount of ten dollars to each and you will get your average amount for your monthly budget. Then deduct the monthly utilities amounts next, water, food and clothing, electricity, and heating expenses. The amount that you have left, you then deduct your transportation expenses. We are prioritizing according to immediate needs. Deduct from what remains the amount of your car note, car insurance, fuel or bus transportation or carpooling. Whatever is left goes to your desires. Such as paying off credit card balances, savings, internet and cell phone bills, entertainment, recreation, saving, and so on.

After developing your monthly budget. You must pray asking God to help you stay within the allocated amounts of your budget, and to help you make wise decisions concerning your spending. If for any reason, you cannot cover priority expenses, you are living outside of your means, and you need to either supplement your income, or downsize. Remember, tithing is honoring the sovereign authority and power of God, enabling the blessing of the Lord to flow in your life. The Lord has blessed me with income enough, for the last 16 years, to pay my monthly expenses on time, never carrying a balance over to the next month, with money left over to give or spend on what I desire, which is not much because I have learned contentment. I have what I desire in my heart, which is to know God in an intimate and personal way.

Along with teaching me to trust, the Lord helped me create a financial system, which will later be introduced.

Keep in mind that change begins from the inside out. This is the key: surrender. If we do not trust God, the second step will be difficult. God has to change our whole perspective, and perception. Paul says in Romans 12:1-2:

I beseech you therefore, brethren, by the

106

mercies of God, that you present your bod-
ies a living sacrifice, holy, acceptable unto
God, which is your reasonable service. And
be not conformed to this world: but be ye
transformed by the renewing of your mind,
that ye may prove what is that good, and
acceptable, and perfect will of God.

We must understand that it is about God's will, and not our will. God's will is good, acceptable, and perfect. The word prove means to try or test. This same word prove, is used also in Malachi 3:10, when God says:

Bring ye all the tithes into the storehouse,
that there may be meat in mine house, and
prove me now herewith, saith the LORD of
hosts, if I will not open you the windows of
heaven, and pour you out a blessing, that
there shall not be room enough to receive it.

Notice, that blessing does not say blessings. God is speaking of pouring out divine favor upon us. Proverbs 10:22 says:

The blessing of the LORD, it maketh rich,
and he addeth no sorrow with it.

The blessing of the Lord is His divine favor. What is the divine favor of the LORD? The divine favor of the LORD is merited, and is given to those who walk upright, or are obedient to the will of God. It is the continual flow of bless ing upon one's life, as the result of walking in the truth of God's word. The divine favor of the LORD is the active word of God, made alive in the believer's life, which bring about all that pleases God. For example, it says in Proverbs 16:7, *"When a man's ways please the LORD, he maketh even his enemies to be at peace with him."*

The child of God who is walking in faith, is pleasing God (Hebrews 11:6). Therefore, the result of him or her walking in faith is what bring about peace and harmony, even among enemies, those who dislike, and despise us simply because God's Spirit is causing us to walk contrary to this world. Their first response to such a person is, that we think we are better than they are. They are in the true sense of the word correct, because we have the divine favor of the LORD upon us. The one that has favor with the LORD, is not the one who has the attitude, it is the one that is not doing the will of God. Now, take every promise of God you believe and manifest those results in your life. It is called walking in the Word, walking in obedience, walking upright or having the divine favor of the LORD, upon us. We are continually being blessed, because the word of God is active, and alive in our life. We are walking in righteousness, peace, and joy in the Holy Ghost. God is ruling and reigning in our heart!

We are the seed of Abraham, and God promises to bless us. In Malachi 3: 6-9, He says,

> *I am the LORD, I change not; therefore ye sons of Jacob are not consumed. Even from the days of your fathers ye are gone away from mine ordinances, and have not kept them. Return unto me, and I will return unto you, saith the LORD of hosts. But ye said, Wherein shall we return? Will a man rob God? Yet ye have robbed me. But ye say, Wherein have we robbed thee? In tithes and offerings. Ye are cursed with a curse: for ye have robbed me, even this whole nation.*

The body of Christ, the present day church, is that nation. This is confirmed in 1 Peter 2:910 which says:

> *But ye are a chosen generation, a royal priesthood, a holy nation, a peculiar people; that ye should show forth the praises of him who hath called you out of darkness into his marvelous light: Which in time past were not a people, but are now the people of God: which had not obtained mercy, but now have obtained mercy.*

You may also reference this context to Romans 11:25-33. We are to return to God by bringing the tithe into the storehouse, or present day place of worship, the church. This is a mark of God, the visible sign that we trust Him.

If you are in debt, you need to develop the budget that takes God's tithe right off the top, living within the other nine tenth, while eliminating your debt altogether. It will take faith and determination. And, you must trust God.

I would like to tell you a story. There cried a certain widow to Elisha, whose husband had died and left her in debt. The creditors where coming to take her two sons in bondage, until the debt was paid off. It says that her husband was one of the sons of the Prophets. Back then the prophet was the spokesperson, or mouthpiece of God. And she knew if her sons were taken in bondage, she would not have a livelihood.

So, this widow woman came to Elisha, and shares with him, what was going on. She knew that whatever was spoken from the prophet came directly from God. Back then they trusted the man of God. Elisha asks her a question. What have you in the house? And she replies, your handmaid has not anything in the house except a pot of oil. It must not have been of any significance, because of the tone of her voice.

Section III - Steps To Financial Freedom

The first point is, God expects for us to start with some thing, and that something is the tithe. After hearing her answer, He gives her instructions. He says: *"Go, borrow thee vessels abroad of all thy neighbors, even empty vessels; borrow not a few. And when thou art come in, thou shalt shut the door upon thee and upon thy sons, and shalt pour out into all those vessels, and thou shalt set aside that which is full* (2 Kings 4:3-4).

So she follows the Prophet instructions, and the Bible says:

> *And it came to pass, when the vessels were full, that she said unto her son, Bring me yet a vessel. And he said unto her, [There is] not a vessel more. And the oil stayed* (2 Kings 4:6).

And it said the oil stopped. Then it goes on to say that she came and told the man of God. And he said,

> *... Go, sell the oil, and pay thy debt, and live thou and thy children of the rest* (2 Kings 4:7).

Second point is, that she had a choice to make. She could obey the man of God, or she could disobey the man of God. Obeying the man of God, tells us that she trusted God. Had she not obeyed Elisha, she would have sacrificed her sons and they would have been taken into bondage. If we say we trust God, then we ought to obey Him, because obedience is better than sacrifice (1 Samuel 15:22). Oftentimes God will remove from our lives those things we value over Him. He may some-times allow financial hardship, because of disobedience. So she obeyed the Prophet (2 King 4:1-7). In Malachi 3:10, we fail to see and understand that God challenges us to try, test, or prove Him, and while we are testing, proving God, He says He will rebuke or turn back the devourer from destroying what we have, and whatever else He blesses us with.

The third point is, that God is able because of obedience, to supernaturally pour out His blessing upon us. We can have a continual flow of God's prosperity in our lives. The tithe places in force or in motion the supernatural power of God in the believer's life. It allows the flow of God's blessing to enter into our lives. If you are not tithing, a tenth of your gross income weekly, bi-weekly, or however you get paid, I dare you to begin tithing, and trusting God. The moment you do, you can expect by faith God's divine favor. He will liberally allow you to see Him blessing you more abundantly, and you will know it is God. God is looking for consistency in our obedience.

Our spiritual walk is not consistent. We are like roller coasters, up one day and down another day. We must grow so that we can rejoice, rejoice always in the Lord. We must walk in holiness, and come out from among the course of this world that is corrupt through the lust that is in it. It's called sanctification, which results in holiness. Sanctification begins with the heart, and inward commitment to God. We are given the responsible of sanctifying ourselves (2 Corinthians 6:14-18). And it is a work of the Holy Spirit (1 Thessalonians 5:23). We are to no longer be conforming to the worldly system of thinking and conduct. Our minds need to be transformed and renewed by the word of God (Romans 12:1-2). God wants us to submit to his authority. God wants us to honor Him, and give Him the glory He is due.

Disobedience in any form hinders the true blessings of God. Our obedience to God should, and was taught to many of us as children growing up in church. We then decide as adults to stray away from God. We must learn that every aspect of our lives is in the will of God. The plans God has for our lives involves our social, economical, and educational lives. We are children of God, and are to be led by the Holy Spirit, who is our helper. We are to follow the guidance and directions of the Lord, as we seek Him in our giving, prayer, and fasting. Trusting His Divine Providence!

✝

—9—

Step Three - Giving

Every man according as he purposeth in his heart, so let him give; not grudgingly, or of necessity: for God loveth a cheerful giver (2 Corinthians 9:7).

Giving is the third step to becoming financially suc cessful from a Biblical perspective. Giving requires a giving heart. A heart that is not selfish. Give means to contribute to some cause. I believe giving is a yardstick to our spiritual growth, and that it measures our spiritual maturity. When we give according to the word of God, we say to God, I trust and have faith in You. The scripture above says that we are to purpose in our hearts what to give. Paul tells us to reach a decision on what we are going to give. Then give it not grudgingly, or of necessity, because God loves a cheerful giver. After we have given God the tithe, along with an offering to which we have purposed in our heart. Now, what ever else we give to the church is called sacrificial giving. We are now giving from an intended purpose.

For example, we have in our budget an allowance for clothing, and the church is assessing you money for Women's or Men's Day. Rather than spending it all on clothing that month, you use from it to pay your assessment. I have experienced favor and many blessings from this type of giving. I give God what belongs to Him, and as I am led by God to give. I obey Him. When making out your budget, allocate an account which you call personal allowance. It is from this account or other accounts that you would give sacrificially, because you are denying what will otherwise go to your pleasures, or other expenses.

The Bible gives us clear instructions on how to give, and the results of our giving. Scriptures say in Matthew 6:1-4,

> *Take heed that ye do not your alms before men, to be seen of them: otherwise ye have no reward of your Father which is in heaven. Therefore when thou doest thine alms, do not sound the trumpet before thee, as the hypocrites do in the synagogues and in the streets, that they may have glory of men. Verily I say unto you, They have their reward. But when thou doest alms, let not thy left hand know what the right hand doeth: That thine alms may be in secret: and thy Father which seeth in secret himself shall reward thee openly.*

Our motive for giving should not be to be seen, or to please men. But, we should give to please God, and when giving is done in faith, God is well pleased. The Bible says that God will openly reward us. When we give to be recognized, we have already received our reward, and it does not please God. Giving should be done in secret. We are not to put on a show. But, some preachers who should know the word of God still insist on lining people up to give, according to the amount of money they want them to give.

When giving an offering other than specifically to the church. For example, giving a love offering for a speaker. You would not place it in an envelope. But rather give it freely, as you purpose in your heart to give. One reason for doing it this way, is because you want to be obedient to the teaching of Christ concerning giving when He said not to let your right hand know, what your left hand is doing. God is pleased because you gave it in secret and cheerfully, knowing that God will reward you. This is giving beyond the tithe and the offerings to the church. So in your heart, you are able to give in secret regardless of man's need is to know.

Almsgiving, which we now call the benevolent fund or offering to the church, is to be used also toward the poor and needy in the church. When I give the offering along with the tithe, I then place it in an envelope, so that the church, in the balancing of the expenditures, may keep financial records. Also, I was shown by God how to overcome the feeling of not being able to give, when in fact, I have given already what is required of me. Now, when I have given what is required of me, which is the tithe and offering to the church, the feeling of not having to give, as I desire, does not overwhelm me. I give what I have. And often time, on Sunday when I go to another church, it is what I have left in my purse. I have learned that any money I purpose not to give, not to put it in my purse, because I will give it all!

I remember the times when God was testing my faith in giving. God would speak to my heart to give a certain amount. This is when I carried a checkbook with me. Since computer checking has arrived, all my banking is done on the computer, except cash withdrawals. I would first calcu late in my mind what money I had, what would happen if I gave it, and whether it could be replaced before something was due. Those were the times God was really dealing with me in my giving. They were the time that I learned to distinguish the voice of God. And hearing, in spite of the toiling of my will, in the end I obeyed and would always be blessed of God.

The Holy Spirit is the one who speaks to us concerning the things of God, and when we refuse to honor God with the tithe, we are disobedient, and this is sin. Jesus tells us that the Holy Spirit would bring us into all truth, and that He would convict us of sin (John 3:21). We can know the word of God. Yet, remain in our sins, simply because we refuse to surrender our wills to God. We want to live according to our ways, and not how the Bible teaches us to live. The attitude in which we give says a lot about whether we trust or not trust God. When we give in obedience, not thinking of ourselves, we are saying to God that we trust Him to replenish that which has been given to us.

God shapes our attitudes by blessing us according to our obedience.   Later on in my walk with God, I came to understand that giving is a gift. The Apostle Paul says:

> *Having then gifts differing according to the grace that is given us, whether prophecy, let us prophesy according to the proportion of faith; Or ministry, let us wait on our ministering: or he that teacheth, on teaching; Or he that exhorteth, on exhortation: he that giveth, let him do it with simplicity (liberality); he that ruleth, with diligence; he that showeth mercy, with cheerfulness* (Romans 12:6-8).

Giving is a gift, and God knows the heart of a giver. When we give ourselves to others we show forth the love of God. Giving is not just money. It is giving of our time, and talents. Giving is when we take the time and talk to others about God, and how He will help them if only they would trust Him. It is taking someone to the market that is not driving. It is giving information about a job to someone seeking employment. Giving is helping someone who is in need, and providing that need. It does not matter what it is, because we are the vessels that God uses to pour out His love to others. He knows He can but speak, and the needs of those who are seeking Him are met. It is you and I that will help others come to know Jesus Christ, because of the love we show in giving of ourselves to them.

God entrusts his resources, or riches, with believers who have learned or exercised their gift of giving. Jesus says in Luke 16:10-12,

He that is faithful in that which is least is faithful also in much: and he that is unjust in the least is unjust also in much. If therefore, ye have not been faithful in the unrighteous mammon, who will commit to your trust the true riches? And if ye have not been faithful in that which is another man's, who shall give you that which is your own?

Jesus would sometimes answer a question with a question. So in doing likewise, this is my question to you: Who can trust someone, who does not trust them?

In our ministering to the needs of others, we must understand that we are instruments of God's righteousness, and that the Holy Spirit resides in us. We must seek God daily, so that He will enable us to minister to the needs of others, by word or deeds. We must understand that the poor or the needy will always be with us. We are not to judge neither have respect of persons. Rather rich or poor. We are to embrace all. James 2:5 says:

Hearken, my beloved brethren, Hath not God chosen the poor of this world rich in faith, and heirs of the kingdom which he hath promised to them that love him?

God is calling the poor who are rich in faith. God is going to move on their faith, and cause them to prosper in their love and obedience to His word. God wants to multiply what you have, as with the widow whose husband left her in debt. God wants you to return to Him, and to trust Him in these economic times of trouble. If you are a child of God, you are under the economy of God!

✝

Epilogue

Bonus Prophetic Teaching from the Author

These Last Days

These Last Days

So teach us to number our days, that we may apply our hearts unto wisdom (Psalm 90:12).

With so much deception in the world, we must seek the whole counsel of God. We must begin to seek God for wisdom, knowledge, and understanding, so as not to be taken by the sleight and trickery of men. For many false teachers and prophets are in the world today.

It was in 2007, that I first got wind of the "Doctrine of the Government of Twelve," and the cell group concepts. The doctrine of the "Government of 12" is to duplicate Christ in the earth. The cell group doctrine is to establish groups in houses, then on Sunday come together in the church to celebrate. I never had heard of these concepts before. I became very alarmed, when the cell group concept was brought into our church when a new pastor replaced our former pastor, and our congregations merged together, and he began to implement the cell group concept in the church. I immediately began to pray and seek God concerning this matter, and this is what I was shown by God.

The original concept is to train leaders, and secure a host/house where you place each leader to teach from written scripts to those who the host brings into their home. The object is to show care, attention, and love to them, which some kind of food or refreshments are involved. Once you have won their trust, and they accept Christ, you invite them into the church. Seems very harmless, but the concept dealt with the emotions of an individual, and not the spirit. Once into the church, emphasis is placed on music, worship, and

118

an experience with God. The original concept says, "give as little word as possible, because the study of scripture is boring to many seeking God. So we will make our churches *"Seeker Friendly."* The concept places emphasis on church growth, and not so much on spiritual growth. The problem here is deception, and then wrong motives. Many were being deceived through emotionalism. The concept is short sighted, with a hidden agenda of creating a religious world government. The concepts come from men high in power, who teachings have reached all the way down to the local churches.

Growth for growth sake should not be the motives, neither should the use of emotionalism or any other type of deceptive tactics. God is real, and there is only one way to Him, and that's through Jesus Christ, His only begotten Son. We must again come to the place where we reverently fear God. To be a true Christian is not always a piece of cake, meaning it is not always sweet. God is not mocked, the problems, deception and wrong motives will come to light.

It was also in 2007, that God began to show me that many small churches, which were struggling to survive. It is these churches God wants this message to reach. That they are not to follow the world's deceptive teaching and practices, they are to trust and obey Him, to remain steadfast in the Lord, and He will bless their obedience.

These concepts were made known through conferences, and the model of these concepts was widely made available on web sites, along with material on how to implement them in local churches.

It was implied that if local pastors did not comply, their churches would be left behind with shrinking congregations. This, however, is not the truth. The local church can and will grow according to God's pre-established plan by implementing the biblical concepts of evangelism by equipping the saints through spiritual growth.

Section IV - Epilogue

David was a man after God's own heart. So must the church be in these last days. Mega Church is not the title you should crave, but to be called a "Church after God's Heart."

A church after God's heart will accomplish growth through the Biblical concepts of evangelism and discipleship by focusing on spiritual growth not church growth.

Some pastors were using the whole model of the cell group concept, while others were using just certain principles. I really did not understand what my former pastor was saying when he stood in the pulpit and made this statement about what one minister meant on television when he said: "We are going to put small churches out of business." Unaware that some of the sheep in their congregations have strayed from the faith, which no longer wanted to hear sound doctrine. The apostle Paul told Timothy to:

> *Preach the word; be instant in season, out of season; reprove, rebuke, exhort with all longsuffering and doctrine. For the time will come when they will not endure sound doctrine; but after their own lusts shall they heap to themselves teachers, having itching ears; And they shall turn away their ears from the truth, and shall be turned unto fables. But watch thou in all things, endure afflictions, do the work of an evangelist, make full proof of thy ministry* (2 Timothy 4:2-5).

2 Peter 2:1-3; 10-11 says:

> *But there were false prophets also among the people, even as there shall be false teachers among you, who privily shall bring in damnable heresies, even denying the Lord that bought them, and bring upon themselves swift destruction. And many shall follow*

their pernicious ways; by reason of whom
the way of truth shall be evil spoken of. And
through covetousness shall they with feigned
words make merchandise of you: whose
judgment now of a long time lingereth not,
and their damnation slumbereth not.

As you continue to read this passage of scripture, you
will find the judgment of God upon the angels that sinned,
the ungodly upon the earth that did not repent before the
flood, the judgment upon Sodom and Gomorrah, which was
destroyed because of homosexuality, and I believe, if we do
not change the United States is heading in that same direction. The scripture that stands out the most is,

The Lord knoweth how to deliver the godly
out of temptations, and to reserve the unjust
unto the day of judgment to be punished:
But chiefly them that walk after the flesh in
the lust of uncleanness, and despise govern-
ment, Presumptuous are they, self-willed,
they are not afraid to speak evil of dignities.
Where as angels, which are greater in pow-
er and might, bring not railing accusation
against them before the Lord.

Birds of a feather flock together!

Not all large churches have implemented these concepts.
They have become large through equipping the saints to go
and share the gospel of Jesus Christ, and through their outreach ministries. The Bible tells us,

That we [henceforth] be no more children,
tossed to and fro, and carried about with
every wind of doctrine, by the sleight of

*men, [and] cunning craftiness, whereby
they lie in wait to deceive;   But speaking
the truth in love, may grow up into him in
all things, which is the head, [even] Christ*
(Ephesians 4:14-15).

*For such [are] false apostles, deceitful work-
ers, transforming themselves into the apostles of Christ.   And no marvel; for Satan
himself is transformed into an angel of light.
Therefore [it is] no great thing if his ministers also be transformed as the ministers of
righteousness; whose end shall be according
to their works* (2 Corinthians 11:13-15).

The Bible places emphasis on spiritual growth, resulting in church growth in the fourth chapter of Ephesians. No human being, or group of people, can take the place of Jesus Christ on earth. It is plain from scripture that the Holy Spirit, and not the apostles did that (John 14:25-26)!   Yet, this is what some church governments today are all about. The hidden agenda is rulership. We are a body, and function as members, not cells! The hidden danger behind these doctrines of men is that they have ushered into the church greed and covetousness. They have ushered into the church another gospel, and not the gospel of the Kingdom of God. This gospel of prosperity is being preached, and has caused many of God's people to remain comfortably in their sins. This gospel is causing many to pursue after the blessings, and not God. The deception in the church today is covetousness—lovers of money.

In 1 Timothy 6:5-10, and 2 Timothy 3:10-13, the apostle Paul warns Timothy to withdraw from men, who he says have corrupt minds, and are destitute of the truth, supposing that gain is godliness. And, that these evil men and imposters will wax worse, and worse, deceiving, and being deceived.

Paul tells Timothy that godliness with contentment is great gain.

> *For we brought nothing into this world, and it is certain we can carry nothing out. And having food and raiment let us be therewith content. But they that will be rich fall into temptation and a snare, and into many foolish and hurtful lusts, which drown men in destruction and perdition. For the love of money is the root of all evil: which while some coveted after, they have erred from the faith, and pierced themselves through with many sorrows* (1 Timothy 6:11-12).

The apostle Paul tells Timothy to flee from foolish and hurtful lusts and pursue rather after righteousness, godliness, faith, love, patience, and meekness. Paul tells Timothy to fight the good fight of faith, and to lay hold of eternal life, which we who are in Jesus Christ, have been called.

Matthew 28:19-20 is where the concept is being taken from, which says:

> *Therefore go and make disciples of all nations.*

But the verse is misinterpreted to mean that all "nations" are to be "discipled" or brought under the control of a religious world government headed up by apostles and prophets. In reality, Jesus sent out his followers to spread the gospel message that would result in individual people from out of all nations receiving Him and becoming Christians, emphasis being placed on "of all nations." In Acts 2:41-47, scripture does teach that they did,

...continuing daily with one accord in the temple, and breaking bread from house to house, did eat their meat with gladness and singleness of heart, Praising God, and having favour with all people. And the Lord added to the church daily such as should be saved.

When interpreted rightfully, it means that they assembled in the temple to be taught, and were given toward hospitality, one to another from house to house, as a community. Another scripture that backs this up is Acts 5:11-14. Solomon's porch was a part of the temple where the apostles did many signs and wonders. Paul says in 1 Corinthians 3:6-7,

I have planted, Apollos watered; but God gave the increase.

Those called to leadership, who were responsible for the care and attention of those who had given their life to Jesus Christ, were called Deacons, in Acts 6:1-4. Persecution is what caused Christians to have church in their houses.

The concept is an example of the workers of iniquity who say that the apostles and the prophets are the true leaders of the church. In 2 Corinthians 11:13-15, the apostle Paul warns the Church at Corinth of false leaders saying:

For such are false apostles, deceitful workers, transforming themselves into the apostles of Christ. And no marvel; for Satan himself is transformed into an angel of light. Therefore it is no great thing if his ministers also be transformed as the ministers of righteousness; whose end shall be according to their works.

Scripture lets us know that satan transforms himself as

an angel of light, and how much more will his ministers.

We need to remember that Christ gave gifts to the church for the edifying of the body of Christ, till we all come into the unity of the faith. We were at one point, divided by denominations. We now see the church unifying. Ephesians 4:11-16 says,

> **[Christ Himself]** *gave some, apostles; and some, prophets; and some, evangelists; and some, pastors and teachers; For the perfecting of the saints, for the work of ministry, for the edifying of the body of Christ; till we all come in the unity of the faith, and of the knowledge of the Son of God, unto a perfect (mature) man, unto the measure of the stature of the fullness of Christ: That we henceforth be no more children, tossed to and fro, and carried about with every wind of doctrine, by the sleight of men, and cunning craftiness, whereby they lie in wait to deceive; But speaking the truth in love, may grow up in all things into him in all things, which is the head, even Christ: From whom the whole body fitly joined together and compacted by that which every joint supplieth,* **[not cell]** *according to the effectual working in the measure of every part, maketh increase the body unto the edifying of itself in love.*

Popularity is not always right. Matthew 7:13-14 says:

> *Enter ye in at the strait gate: for wide is the gate, and broad is the way, that leadeth to destruction, and many there be which go in thereat: Because strait is the gate, and*

narrow is the way, which leadeth unto life, and few there be that find it: Beware of false prophets, which come to you in sheep's clothing, but inwardly they are ravening wolves.

These concepts are called non-traditional evangelism. Wherefore, the traditional evangelism in the Bible for the church is lifestyle, witnessing door-to-door, one-on-one, and in the assembly (Matthew 5:16; Luke 9:1-6; Acts 8:34-39; Acts 2:14-41).

In spite of man's methods, God's Word prevails, Isaiah 55:6-11 says:

"Seek ye the LORD while he may be found, call ye upon him which he is near: Let the wicked forsake his way, and the unrigh-teousness man his thoughts: and let him return unto the LORD, for he will abundantly pardon. For my thoughts are not your thoughts, neither are your ways my ways saith the LORD. God' word further explains, "For as the heavens are higher than the earth, so are my ways higher than your ways, and my thoughts than your thoughts. For as the rain cometh down, and the snow from the heaven, and returneth not thither, but waterth the earth, and maketh it bring forth and bud, that it may give seed to the sower, and bread to the eater: So shall my word be that goeth out of my mouth: it shall not return unto me void, but it shall prosper in the thing whereto I sent it."

These scriptures tell us that in spite of the motive behind the preaching or teaching of God's Word, it will accomplish its attended end, to save those who hear, believe, and obey.

Beware, the deception in the church today is covetousness. We are to be aware of the direction the Church is heading. The motive behind the cell group concept says, "Grow the Church to dominate the world." But Jesus Christ is returning to take us out of the world, and will establish His physical kingdom reign on the earth, after the tribulation, and during the millennium. After the millennium, Jesus Christ will deliver the kingdom to God the Father, and Jesus will be crowned ruler forever (Revelation 19-22).

The prince of the power of the air, (satan) the spirit that is now at work in the children of disobedience, uses mammon, the personification of wealth or riches; to take men captive by its power. I rather obey God, than man (Acts 5:29). Repent, for the Kingdom of God is at hand!

I rather obey God, than man (Acts 5:29)!

✝

Contact:

You may call (313) 231-6836 or send your prayer request to:

Francine Shaw Ministries
P.O. Box 03237
Highland Park, MI 48203

or

Send to e-mail address
francineshawministries@yahoo.com

Please include contact information...Thank you!

About the Author

Francine Shaw is an Intercessor, Teacher and an Evangelist of New World Community Church, Detroit, Michigan. She is a certified member of International Chaplaincy Training Inc., where she serves as an Ordained Community Chaplain. She has been in ministry for 40 years, which 10 years were in recovery, deliverance, and spiritual growth, and 30 years was training.

Her biblical perspective comes from her knowledge of God, and her actual experience of trusting and walking in the truth of God's Word. She is a Gulf War Veteran, and served in the Army National Guard for 11 years. God used her military training to teach her spiritual warfare, which enabled her to overcoming self, the practice of sin, and the strategies of the devil. Her God given vision is to establish an educational facility for the people of God for the purpose of spiritual growth and leadership development.

Francine Shaw contributes her leadership development to the Late J. C. Powell, Founder of New World Community Church. The Late Bishop William Hamilton France Sr., who ordained and trained her in the preaching of the Gospel of Jesus Christ, and Pastor Nathaniel Cotton Sr., who trained her in the Pastoral Ministries. A ll are great men of God.

To order additional copies of *Wisdom for Financial Success* or to find more life changing books by *Acts Publishing*, please Contact:

Outreach at *Acts Publishing*
P.O. Box 03600
Highland Park, MI 48203
actspublishing@yahoo.com

Or call (313) 231-6836

Special discounts are available for ministry, academic, retail or fundraising purposes.